FERNS FOR GARDEN
AND GREENHOUSE

FERNS

FOR

GARDEN

AND

GREENHOUSE

Philip Swindells

LONDON
J. M. DENT & SONS LTD

First published 1971
© Philip Swindells 1971

Made in Great Britain
at the
Aldine Press · Letchworth · Herts
for
J. M. DENT & SONS LTD
Aldine House · Bedford Street · London

ISBN: 0 460 03983 0

CONTENTS

ILLUSTRATIONS

Between pages 22 and 23

Epiphytic, warm-greenhouse, fern: *Platycerium
    coronarium*
Photograph by the author
Moisture-loving,   hardy   fern: *Matteuccia
    struthiopteris*
Epiphytic, warm-greenhouse, fern *Asplenium
    nidus*
Photograph by the author
Moisture-loving fern: *Osmunda regalis*

Between pages 38 and 39

Shade-loving ferns:
    Blechnum spicant
    Athyrium filix-femina plumosum
Moisture-loving *Thelypteris palustris* growing in
    marsh

Between pages 54 and 55

Moisture-loving fern: *Onoclea sensibilis*
The shade-loving *Athyrium filix-femina*
The shade-loving *Polystichum setiferum*
A cool-greenhouse fern, *Cyrtomium falcatum*
A rock garden fern, *Gymnocarpium dryopteris*

Between pages 70 and 71

Cool-greenhouse ferns:
    Pteris ensiformis evergemiensis
    Pteris cretica albolineata
Cool-greenhouse fern: *Pteris serrulata*
    'Cristata'
Warm-greenhouse fern: *Platycerium alcicorne*

Unless otherwise stated all the photographs are
    by Mr P. R. Chapman, A.R.P.S.

vii

INTRODUCTION

There cannot be a group of plants either more maligned or overlooked than the hardy ferns. Few gardens would not be improved by the addition of some of these amenable subjects, yet since the great Victorian fern era they seem to have been ignored by gardeners and nurserymen alike. Unfortunately many of the extremely fine named varieties grown by our grandparents were irretrievably lost during the First World War and this has possibly been a contributing factor in their decline in popularity. Nowadays, however, despite the lack of improved garden varieties, there are still enough species and forms in cultivation to enable the gardener to transform a shady corner into an interesting and peaceful haven.

Greenhouse species have suffered similarly, but it is evident that with the current trend of apartment dwelling that house plants will continue to increase in popularity. It is to be hoped that with this awakening, the continual upsurge in the popularity of ferns such as *Nephrolepis* and *Pteris* will lead to greater things, and that one day all the old varieties that were grown so beautifully in Victorian conservatories will reappear, to become as familiar a part of the British living-room as the television set.

This little book, it is hoped, will encourage the gardener who regards one fern as very much like another to look a second time and consider the possibilities of introducing a plant or two into his garden, greenhouse or living-room. I also hope that the gardener with a new-found or established interest in ferns will find some beneficial information in these pages, and that he may be inspired to grow some of the more difficult and temperamental species that may otherwise become lost to cultivation.

Throughout this book I have aimed at simplicity, and with this in mind I would ask the knowledgeable reader and purist to bear with me when I refer to a popular plant by what may now be an outdated name. Whilst fully appreciating the reasons for the changing of names, I feel that in an introduction to the cultivation of ferns it is better to retain certain of the older and popular names, which incidentally are still used by the majority of nurserymen.

1

Introducing Ferns

To the layman a fern is usually any green plant with attractive, much divided, foliage. Confusion therefore arises when he is told that the Asparagus 'Fern' is not in fact a fern but a very close relative of the Lily, and that when referring to the Flowering Fern (Osmunda) he is using contradictory terms.

All ferns, together with Horse-tails and Clubmosses, belong to a large group of flowerless plants known as the Pteridophyta. They are, in the main, plants from the Devonian Period, approximately 400 million years ago, a time when coal was being formed and the first amphibians were crawling onto the land. Over this wide span of time they have changed little, so that those which we now cultivate in our gardens are in all probability the same as the ones which colonized the forests and moorland areas in the age of dinosaurs and similar prehistoric creatures.

In many respects they are similar to flowering plants, having well-developed leaves and roots, and a structure consisting mainly of woody fibre. But striking differences are apparent when their reproductive processes are compared. That of a fern is described fully in the chapter on propagation; briefly it consists of the production of spores from which arise independent organisms responsible for the sexual elements. This differs markedly from the seed of a flowering plant, which on sowing immediately produces a completely independent, self-contained plant.

In common with the more sophisticated flowering plants, the fern consists essentially of stem, leaf and root. The stem normally bears leaves at the top and roots at the base. In some species the stem is very short, with leaves crowded upon it, whilst in others it is horizontal, often underground, and bears leaves and roots at varying intervals along its length, although

1

new foliage is always produced from the extremities of the main stem or its branches.

Every fern has a stem, even if it may not at first be very evident. In some it is quite short and described as a rootstock, whereas in others it is long and trailing and known as a rhizome. In many species of the tree ferns it appears in its most exaggerated form as a tall thick fibrous trunk.

The stem of a fern is much simpler in structure than that of a typical flowering plant, and does not have the same bark or hard outer protective covering. Instead it is often clothed in hairs or scales, or a combination of both. These thickly cover the tender growing-point and often persist for much of the year, forming an additional attraction in the garden.

Arising from the stem is the leafy portion, or frond. Usually this is lance-shaped or oval and consists of what we might loosely term a stem or stalk from which the leaflets, or pinnae, radiate. This stalk is more correctly called a stipe and often bears persistent scales or hairs like those of the rhizome. It acts very much like the main vein in a leaf, supporting the attractive leafy portions which carry the sporangia, or spore-bearing bodies.

These appear as small black or brown mounds of dust, and in most cases are borne on the undersides of the fronds, either in neat rows or scattered between the veins. Some species produce both barren and fertile fronds, and the spores are then usually carried in extensive terminal clusters on the fertile portions.[1]

The position of these fruiting bodies in relation to the leaf veins and other similar features is of the utmost importance in the identification and classification of various species. And in view of the tremendous differences between flowering and non-flowering plants, perhaps a word or two here on general plant classification and the outline of fern identification methods would not come amiss.

To whatever part of the vegetable kingdom a plant belongs, it is always placed under the collective heading of a genus. Each genus is a group of individual plants in which the principal

[1] See also Chapter 3.

characteristics are alike, e.g. *Dryopteris*. Within this genus there are individual species. All the plants in the genus belong to one or other species, for these are composed of plants in which all the important, more detailed, characteristics are the same. Therefore all plants of one species are given a specific name, which in simple terms may be likened to our own Christian name, the generic name taking the place of the surname but with the word order reversed thus, *Dryopteris filix-mas*.

Sometimes plants of the same species which have evolved in different parts of the world show differences in size, colouring, texture, etc., which remain stable even under garden conditions. These are referred to as varieties of a species thus, *Dryopteris filix-mas* var. *paleacea*.

Forms created either deliberately or accidentally by man are termed cultivars, e.g. *Dryopteris filix-mas* 'Jervisii'. Whilst those resulting from a cross with another species in their natural habitat are known as natural hybrids, *Dryopteris* × *traveli* (*Dryopteris borreri* × *Dryopteris filix-mas*).

The actual naming and placing of a plant in one of the categories mentioned depends upon structural factors, some of which may require a hand lens to see and verify. But as in flowering plants, the broad principles of classification are based upon the position, size and shape of their fertile parts. In ferns these consist of spores, sporangia and sori, and although the separating out of plants according to these structures is a useful starting point, it is by no means final and conclusive evidence of a particular fern's true identity, and therefore other more remote and complex characters have to be studied carefully.

In short, a gardener who is capable of using a flora (a book containing a key to the identity of plants by their structure) can identify an unnamed fern with reasonable accuracy, probably near enough for his particular needs, but the more advanced plantsman will have considerable difficulty in sorting out various sub-species and variants within the collective complex of one species unless he is prepared to delve into the intricacies of chromosomes. In which case he will cease to be a gardener and will become a botanist.

2

Cultivation

Ferns seldom pose the gardener any significant cultural problems. Indeed, it might be said that provided common sense is applied during the various stages of growth, even the non-gardener confronted with these subjects for the first time could produce plants of reasonable appearance.

The hardy species are usually grown in a shady border or, in the case of the more diminutive kinds, on the rock garden.

In a border they are treated along broadly similar lines to those of their more familiar flowering herbaceous counterparts. The site selected should be at least partially shaded, with a northerly aspect if possible, and of good clean friable loam. Although moisture is important, the ground should be well drained and not allowed to become stagnant. Ideal soil conditions can be created by digging to a good spade depth and incorporating liberal quantities of peat moss (the coarse kind known as tailings) and rotted leaves or old manure. If this is done in the early autumn, and the upturned soil is left to the mercy of the elements, it will become an admirable medium in which to plant the ferns during the following February or March.

I always prefer to plant at this time, as I find that autumn planted stock tends to be slow to make a start and often produces much smaller fronds than normal during the first season.

Routine management is the same as normally advocated for ordinary hardy border plants and consists principally of keeping down the weeds and ensuring a constant water supply, especially for newly planted stock. When sufficient suitable material is available, a good mulch around the crowns is beneficial. Old compost, well-rotted manure and leaf-mould are the best and should be spread to about an inch deep around the crowns of the plants.

Gardeners who wish to grow really fine specimen plants, rather than create just a soft blending of foliage, usually have to spend a little more time with their plants in order to employ what is popularly known as the single crown method of culture. This means that the ferns are restricted to one centre of growth and not permitted to form a crowd of offsets. The 'shuttlecock' kinds of ferns, that is those with a circle of fronds around a central core of stem, are very apt to produce young plants from the bases of the fronds outside the circle. If left unrestricted these rapidly assume adult proportions, and in doing so jostle with the parent plant for light, air and root run. This invariably results in the plants becoming dwarfed, while the crowding of the foliage detracts from the individual grace and beauty of the species. A single crown, kept so by the persistent removal of such youngsters, will have fronds double the size and will show off its various varietal characteristics to much greater advantage.

The smaller varieties of hardy fern are more usually grown on the rock garden, although some can be used to advantage at the front of a shady border. Rock garden culture is simple if one takes the trouble to study the preferences of each individual fern. Several for instance will not tolerate the presence of lime in the soil while others seem to revel in conditions where it is plentiful. Some will grow happily in the exposed niches between rocks, whereas their neighbours prefer a cool sheltered position.

Basically there are two points to bear in mind when selecting and planting ferns on a rock garden. Firstly, choose those of suitable stature and temperament for the prevailing conditions, and secondly provide adequate drainage at all times. Before planting, take a good depth of soil from each pocket and place a layer of old clinker or broken pot crocks in the bottom. Mix the excavated soil with lime-free grit, one part grit to five parts soil, and then replace. This provides a reasonable general growing medium in which most species will do well, and of course it can be varied to suit the individual fern by adding a little lime or a handful of peat as the case may be.

Unfortunately a few of the best dwarf hardy ferns cannot be

grown to perfection on the open rock garden. Some, like the Sea Spleenwort (*Asplenium marinum*), require great care with watering and only do well if sprayed overhead several times a day with tepid rainwater. Others produce their fronds much too early and are then either frosted or suffer damage from cold winds. It would be wrong, however, to dismiss these as too difficult to manage, for all respond well to care in the confines of an unheated frame or alpine house.

Unheated is the operative word. I well remember when working for one of the country's leading growers of hardy ferns, forcing some of the beautiful hardy Ostrich Fern (*Matteucia struthiopteris*) in gentle heat in an attempt to have plants with mature fronds ready for the Chelsea Flower Show, held annually each May. They grew well until a couple of weeks before the show, when they were stood outside in pots in a sheltered position in order to prepare them for their draughty ordeal in the marquee. Within a few hours the fronds had collapsed and ultimately they shrivelled. This was not due solely to being exposed to cooler air, for a few of the smaller plants which had remained behind in the greenhouse also outgrew their strength and folded up three or four weeks later. This is something I have never forgotten, and a point worth remembering when starting with hardy ferns under glass.

When growing alpine ferns, I prefer to use half-pots rather than either the conventional clay pots or seed-pans. These provide sufficient depth for accommodating both a layer of old crocks and a reasonable amount of soil. Again the particular likes and dislikes of the varieties grown should be learnt before planting, but apart from this, routine operations are confined to shading the plants from intense sunlight and spraying overhead daily with clear water. I like to use rainwater whenever possible because tap water invariably leaves an unsightly limy deposit on the foliage after a period of some three or four weeks.

Cool greenhouse culture is very similar, but in this case the greenhouse is usually heated sufficiently to keep out the frost. As few gardeners are prepared to turn their greenhouse over entirely to the cultivation of ferns, they will normally have to be grown in pots on, or beneath, the staging rather than in borders, as was the custom in our grandparents' time. Composts vary from plant to plant, but the basic potting technique is the same. Fill the bottom of a suitably sized pot with old pot crocks and then cover with a layer of coarse peat. Place the compost on top of this until the pot is about half full and then firm it down well. Add the remaining compost, working it in and around the roots of the plant, which should be held centrally in the pot. Firm this down, leaving half an inch or so of pot-rim above the level of the soil to allow for watering, and then give the plant a thorough soaking.

It will depend upon the variety as to where it will grow best, but I like to mix my ferns amongst the gaudy colours of the Geraniums and Fuchsias, and whenever possible to clothe the area beneath the staging in cool, refreshing, green growth.

Some varieties, both in the warm- and cool-greenhouse section, grow admirably in hanging baskets, particularly the Ladder Ferns (*Nephrolepis*), which are often grown in this manner commercially. The wire basket frame is lined with green sphagnum moss, a layer of drainage material placed in the bottom, and then the plants and compost are introduced in the normal way. Generally speaking more than one plant is required in each basket, but it is imperative that these be of the same variety or else they will cascade over the sides at different rates and create an unbalanced and ugly spectacle.

The method of growing warm-greenhouse ferns is virtually identical with that already described for cool-greenhouse cultivation, except that the temperature is obviously much higher and in most cases the plants require considerable shade from the direct rays of the sun. When ferns are the sole occupants of the greenhouse it is beneficial to keep the paths damped down with a hosepipe, and to administer gentle overhead sprays of water to the foliage both morning and night, especially during the summer months.

Perhaps a word or two here on the cultivation of epiphytic ferns, particularly the Stag's-horn Ferns (*Platycerium*), would not come amiss in view of the fact that they are almost exclusively warm-greenhouse plants. As they live entirely on the branches of trees in their wild state, the gardener must obviously do his best to simulate similar conditions in his greenhouse. The usual method for epiphytes is to attach them to a piece of log or Osmunda fibre and suspend them from the greenhouse roof, although I have seen elaborate arrangements consisting of a substantial tree branch fastened securely to the ground and covered with epiphytic ferns, orchids and bromeliads, which cling tenaciously from each cleft in the branch. Planting, if we might refer to it as that, consists of wrapping the roots of the plant in a leafy compost enclosed by green sphagnum moss and then wiring them to a log or piece of Osmunda fibre. The entire 'package' is then given a thorough soaking and suspended from the greenhouse roof. It must be watched carefully for the first few weeks and watered regularly. After a short time it will become attached to its host and the wires can be removed. Thereafter see that it does not go short of water and you will have a fascinating display that will give you immense pleasure for many years.

Having completed the broad outline of cultivation under glass, I must just mention the possibilities of tender ferns as house plants for those who are not fortunate enough to possess a greenhouse. Potting methods and routine cultivation obviously still hold true, but many people seem to find it difficult to keep ferns happy in the warm dry atmosphere of the living-room. The easiest way of overcoming this problem is to create a mini-atmosphere in the immediate vicinity of the plant. Take the pot and stand it in an empty one of a larger size, and then place in a clay saucer. Pack the gap between the two pots with moist sphagnum moss. Fill the saucer with water and see that the moss is kept continually damp. This ensures a high humidity in the immediate proximity of the plant and leads to vastly improved growth.

Occasionally a fern that is growing quite happily in the house will suddenly shrivel and die. The cause is usually traced to the presence of a minute quantity of unburnt household gas in the atmosphere. I am afraid there is little that can be done to save such a plant, for the fronds of all indoor ferns are very delicate and sensitive.

3

Propagation

There are several different methods of propagating ferns, but by far the most usual is the raising of spores. Many gardeners seem to think that this is difficult. Nothing, however, could be further from the truth. Provided a little of their life history is understood, and conditions are provided in accordance with their basic requirements, success is almost assured.

Spores are not, as is commonly believed, the fern's equivalent of seed, but are comparable with the pollen grains of a flowering plant. The adult fern as we know it is asexual—neuter—and produces clusters of sporangia which contain the spores on the backs of their fronds—or leaves. These appear as mounds of black or brown dust and in nature they rupture, to cast clouds of viable spores into the wind. On reaching a suitable surface they germinate and produce a curious triangular-shaped green scale-like growth called a prothallus. When mature these tiny prothalli develop male and female organs on their undersides. Then the resultant male gametes—or sexual reproductive cells— fertilize the female ones. After this stage the fern as we know it grows and develops with recognizable fronds.

Spores that are ripe and suitable for sowing will disperse as a dusty cloud when the frond is lightly tapped. These can be collected by enclosing the whole, or a sizable portion, of the fertile frond in a large paper bag, breaking the frond stalk, and then upturning it in the bag. Given a vigorous shaking, the ripe spores will detach themselves from the fruiting body and collect in the bottom of the bag. A different bag must be used for each species because some of the dust-like spores will almost certainly remain behind after each operation.

There are several methods of raising spores, but the one which I favour for its cheapness and simplicity works admirably with all the fern species likely to be encountered by the average

9

gardener. Well scrubbed and sterilized clay pans are filled with a sterilized compost of three parts peat, one part loam, and just enough crushed charcoal to keep it sweet. The whole surface area is then covered with a layer of clean, finely crushed brick dust and the spores are sprinkled thinly on this in the same way as one might sow lobelia or begonia seed. A small square of glass is laid over the top of the pan, which is then placed in a saucer of soft water in a warm, partially shaded position in a greenhouse or closed frame. (The soft water may be either rainwater or water that is artificially softened; the former is preferable.)

After about three weeks, depending on variety and temperature, the tiny prothalli will begin to smother the surface of the pan, appearing as a creeping mossy growth. It is imperative at this stage that the saucer be kept continually full of water, for drying out of the soil surface at this crucial time, if only for a few hours, will ruin or greatly reduce the chances of success—fertilization taking place only when there is a film of water on the soil surface.

Eventually minute fronds will appear amidst the mossy growth, and the glass should be removed to allow the air to circulate freely. The young ferns should remain in the pan until they are sufficiently large to handle comfortably, when they can be pricked out in clumps into a compost of equal parts peat and loam and then placed in a cool, moist, airy position. They can remain like this until growing strongly, when they should be lifted and the individual plantlets teased out of the clumps and pricked out singly.

Most varieties are comparatively easy to raise in this manner, but the spores of the various Osmunda species should always be sown immediately after collection, for these contain a small quantity of chlorophyll, which renders them viable for only a few days.

Sometimes one discovers a fern which is notoriously difficult to raise in this manner, particularly among some of the more sophisticated warm-greenhouse species. I have found that many which had earlier failed germinate quite freely if sown on the surface of the fibrous rootstock of an adult growing specimen of the Bird's-nest Fern, *Asplenium nidus*. I now retain a plant or two of this species permanently in my greenhouse for this specific purpose.

In addition to spores, several ferns produce young plantlets or bulbils on their fronds. Notable amongst these are *Asplenium bulbiferum, Cystopteris bulbifera* and several of the *Polystichums*, especially *P. proliferum*. These tiny plants can be collected and planted in boxes of equal parts loam and peat compost and stood in a cool airy position. Thereafter they should be kept moist and treated in the same way as prescribed for young spore-raised plants.

Some gardeners find it easier, particularly with *Polystichum proliferum*, to detach the complete adult frond and peg it down on a tray of compost, securing it with hair-grips or wire staples. In this way the young plants are not subjected to quite the same shock, and seem to root more readily. When well rooted they are easily detached from the old frond by severing the persistent mid-rib between each young plant.

The Hart's-tongue Fern, *Phyllitis scolopendrium*, and its varieties, exhibit another method of bulbil production which I believe is unique in the fern kingdom. The frond bases of this species remain green and living long after the leafy part of the frond has withered, if they are removed from the plant, washed and cleaned, and then planted in a pan of sandy compost and covered with a sheet of glass. Then, after several weeks, tiny white bulbils will be seen to form on each frond base. They can be pricked out into a compost of equal parts sharp sand, loam and peat, and should be kept covered with a sheet of glass until strong enough to fend for themselves. This method is particularly useful with such varieties as *Phyllitis scolopendrium crispum*, which are normally barren and hitherto could only be propagated by division.

Division, however, does play an important part in building up stocks of many of the very choice varieties of ferns. For instance, nothing raised from a sowing of spores collected from a true plant of *Athyrium filix-femina victoriae* could compete with a plant grown from a division of the original find. As with herbaceous plants, division consists merely of splitting a cluster of growing points into individual self-supporting crowns. Many of the hardy species may be too tough to separate with the hands, in which case two garden forks inserted in the centre of the clump, back to back, and levered one against the other, will usually have the desired effect.

Apart from being readily divisible, several species also produce creeping underground stems, each terminating in a cluster of green knuckle-like buds. In some kinds, such as *Dryopteris dilatata*, the stems are short and thick, and the young plants at the ends will eventually emerge close to the crowns of the parents, but in other cases, such as *Matteucia struthiopteris*, the rhizomes are long and wiry, and new plants may suddenly appear some two or three feet from the original plant.

This rambling habit can be used to advantage when young stock of a particular plant is wanted quickly or in large quantities. The adult crown is lifted, the young underground runners detached close enough to the terminal buds to make them manageable propositions, yet not so close as to put the continued existence of the new plants in jeopardy. These pieces of rhizome are then carefully planted in boxes of equal parts peat and loam compost and treated in much the same manner as advocated for young plants which have been raised from spores.

4

Pests and Diseases

Ferns seem to suffer less from pests and diseases than any other group of plants. This is fortunate, for their fronds are usually very sensitive and inclined to curl up and die when a harsh chemical cure is used on them. Indeed when I was a student at the Cambridge Botanic Gardens we were not allowed to use ordinary D.D.T./Lindane smokes in the conservatory without first covering the fronds of all the ferns with old newspapers. Even then they tended to look unhappy for a day or two after smoking, especially the *Adiantums*. Likewise Karathane and Malathion were used with great care in the stove-house, the fronds of delicate species being swathed in polythene before spraying operations could commence.

Hardy ferns seem to be much tougher, particularly the *Dryopteris* species. Attempts to get rid of the common Male Fern (*Dryopteris filix-mas*), when it has been growing wild in parts of the garden where it is unwanted, by spraying with brushwood killer, have succeeded only in defoliating it; it has come up several times afterwards and required regular spraying before being killed outright. This is in marked contrast to some of the tropical *Adiantums* that will look unhappy if merely sprayed with water that is too hard for their liking.

FERN RUST

This is a fungus disease which occasionally rears its ugly head amongst plants of *Cystopteris*. It usually appears as a rusty deposit beneath the fronds, which eventually become yellow and die. By removing and burning affected foliage the disease can easily be contained.

GREENFLY

The common greenfly sometimes makes an appearance on

13

broad-fronded ferns, especially under glass. They usually congregate beneath the fronds, causing extensive twisting and disfigurement of the foliage. Any good commercial greenfly spray will prevent further trouble, but it should be mixed slightly under strength, and used only in the evening or in a shady part of the greenhouse, in order to prevent excessive damage to the fronds. I always prefer to use a weak chemical two or three times to effect a cure, rather than use a full-strength spray once and defoliate the entire plant.

ROOT-FEEDING MEALY BUG

This species of mealy bug is particularly troublesome on pot-grown ferns. An affected plant will look tired and listless, and on its being knocked out of its pot masses of tiny white bugs surrounded in thread-like wax will be seen nestling amidst the roots. Control of severe attacks consists of shaking the plant free from soil and then immersing the roots in a nicotine solution before repotting in fresh compost. In mild cases it may be sufficient to probe the affected areas with a cocktail stick and spear the pests. But whatever method is adopted it is essential to scald the pots with boiling water before repotting in order to destroy any insects that might be lurking within. The same also applies before storing or re-using pots that have accommodated infested plants.

SCALE INSECTS

These are small hard-coated insects which suck the sap of both hardy and greenhouse ferns. They are practically immobile and resemble small brownish blisters on all parts of the fronds. Apart from looking unsightly, they cause wilting and general listlessness in their hosts, often excreting a sticky substance known as honeydew over the fronds, which usually leads to a secondary attack by the sooty mould fungus.

In cases of severe infestation it is better to cut off all the fronds and give the plants a fresh start, but where only one or two colonies have made an appearance, dabbing the insects with a mild nicotine solution will usually clear up the trouble.

WEEVILS

These are most pernicious and irritating pests, which attack ferns and many other plants both under glass and in the open, although by far the greater damage occurs indoors. The adult beetles are brownish, with distinctive long snouts, and devour the foliage of the more delicate species. But by far the most extensive damage is caused by the larvae which infest the roots, particularly of pot-grown plants. Dusting around the plants with D.D.T. will help control the pests out of doors. Or they can be trapped by screwing up a piece of old newspaper or sacking and leaving it in the immediate vicinity of the plants. The insects will hide in the folds and creases during the day and can be easily shaken out and destroyed.

They can also be dusted with D.D.T. in the greenhouse, or if only a few plants are being grown they can easily be turned out of their pots and all the larvae that are visible picked out with a pointed stick and destroyed. If either treatment is ineffective it would be as well to shake the roots entirely free from the soil and larvae, and then repot the plants in a fresh, uncontaminated compost. An old-fashioned method of control is to group the plants together during the day, standing them on a greased sheet or something similar. Enter the greenhouse at night with a bright light and shake the plants whilst holding them to one side. The adult weevils will fall onto the sticky surface and thus be easily caught.

5

Shade-loving Ferns

Most varieties of hardy fern are regarded as plants exclusively for those shady and awkward positions in the garden where nothing else will grow. While this is the use to which these plants are most frequently put, it would be only fair to say that they will not give of their best in such situations. Therefore the gardener who is contemplating growing ferns as a hobby, rather than as plants for brightening a dreary corner with the minimum of attention, would be well advised to consider each species individually and cherish it as he might his prize Chrysanthemums or Delphiniums. With this in mind, even the rawest novice will have reasonable success with any of the following varieties provided, of course, that he fulfils their basic cultural requirements.

ATHYRIUM

Lady Ferns. Only one hardy species can be regarded as a true woodland plant, the others coming from more open, mountainous locations and being more suited to the rock garden.

A. FILIX-FEMINA

Common Lady Fern. For grace, elegance and tolerance of widely differing situations few ferns can compare with the common Lady Fern. This charming native with its dainty, arching, pale green fronds has been the delight of gardeners for many years, and under the influence of cultivation has given rise to many very attractive and distinct mutations.

The true species is very adaptable and appears to be capable of producing frond forms compatible with the conditions under which it is growing. Indeed in some cases the differences

16

in the structure of the fronds are so great as to mislead one into believing that they belong to plants of entirely different species. However, under good garden conditions of partial shade and ample moisture the fronds are fairly uniform in both size and structure. They grow abundantly from a stout, tufted rootstock, are lance-shaped, very brittle, and attain a height of some three or four feet. The long, slender stipes, or frond stalks, are purplish in colour and support alternate pairs of handsome velvety green leaflets. When the young fronds unfurl during late spring they are thickly clothed in deep rust-red scales and emit a sweet delightful earthy aroma. Unfortunately both of these splendid characteristics are short-lived, the aroma disappearing within a few days of the fronds unfurling, and the scales withering and dropping off after a further two or three weeks. Another shortcoming of this species is the way in which it sheds its fronds prematurely in the autumn, whether or not a frost has occurred. Almost overnight they assume a rich lemon-yellow hue and within a few days have shrivelled away completely, leaving only the tip of the brown tufted rootstock above ground.

Culture is quite easy. A moist position in partial shade is all they ask, together with occasional lifting and replanting of old crowns. This encourages stronger growth, for in many old plants the crown grows right out of the ground, making life extremely difficult for the young roots, therefore replanting at regular intervals helps to revitalize them by putting roots and ground in close proximity. A heavy mulch with old leaves or well-rotted manure will have the same effect, but unfortunately these materials are seldom available in liberal quantities.

Propagation by spores is relatively simple and one always stands a chance of discovering a new form, but in the average garden division of the crowns is likely to be more practical.

Towards the end of the famous Victorian fern era there were no fewer than forty distinct garden varieties of *Athyrium filix-femina* in commerce. Sadly, many of these have been lost to cultivation, but those that have survived are of sound constitution and exhibit many diverse and pleasing habits of growth. The following are some of the more easily obtainable varieties, and the keen gardener who raises his own young plants from spores of these may come up with some that are even more diverse and pleasing to the eye, although, as may be expected, he will raise a lot of worthless material as well.

A. F.-F. CAPUT-MEDUSAE

A small-growing shade-lover of dubious garden merit but of great curiosity value. The leaflets or pinnules form a tightly congested ball at the top of a short, almost naked, stem. Seldom worth growing from spores because many grotesque forms appear that are of absolutely no value. Division is far more satisfactory. (6–9 in.).

A. F.-F. CORONATUM

A compact variety with ordinary uncrested fronds and a heavy terminal tassel. There are many different forms about, mainly from spore-raised stock. (9–18 in.).

A. F.-F. CORYMBIFERUM

Many different forms bear this name, but all are characterized by a large terminal crest that is divided into several groups or bunches. Good forms should be propagated by division. (1–1½ ft.).

A. F.-F. CRAIGII CRISTATUM

The fronds of this variety are of rather unusual appearance, being fairly broad at the base and tapering sharply to the apex, where they branch out into a terminal crest. (1–2 ft.).

A. F.-F. CRISTATUM

The most popular of the crested sorts, with short fronds, rarely exceeding eighteen inches in height, that are crowned with heavy terminal crests of twisted, crimpled leaflets. Propagation by division of the finest forms is recommended.

A. F.-F. FRIZELLIAE

Tatting Fern. An extraordinary plant discovered in Ireland many years ago. The individual pinnae, or leaflets, are reduced to curious little balls, which give the fronds a most unusual appearance. Several different and crested forms have occurred in young plants raised from spores, but on the whole stock grown in this manner is fairly even. (1–1½ ft.).

A. F.-F. MULTIFIDUM

One of the most refined and graceful Lady Ferns. The entire frond is finely cut and surmounted by slender, delicately branched, finger-like crests. (1 ft.).

A. F.-F. PLUMOSUM

Pale green, wispy and feathery fronds of exceptional beauty. Many named selections of this form are available and decidedly superior to the common sort. Spores produce interesting variations, but the best varieties should be grown from divisions. (1–3 ft.).

A. F.-F. VICTORIAE

To my mind this is the most outstanding variety of all. Found close on a century ago, allegedly under a hedgerow in central Scotland, this form produces fronds of a similar size and nature to those of the species, except that the pinnae or leaflets are attractively crested and cross one another in an almost religiously symbolic manner. Many forms of this are currently in circulation, mostly raised from spores, but it is doubtful whether few if any really measure up to the excellent form exhibited by those obtained from divisions of the original find. (1½–3½ ft.).

BLECHNUM

Handsome evergreen ferns for a lime-free soil. They make an excellent foil for brightly coloured bulbous subjects such as Liliums and Narcissus.

B. SPICANT

Hard Fern. Striking native with narrow, dark green, leathery barren fronds some two feet long. The fertile ones are slightly larger, covered in extensive fructifications and stand erect from the centre of the plant. Many different varieties have been recorded but these are seldom encountered in cultivation. Propagation by spores, although slow, is comparatively easy. (1–2½ ft.).

B. TABULARE

(*Lomaria magellanica*). A real old favourite. Like a much larger version of *B. spicant*, but with everything more neatly and symmetrically arranged around the crown. (2–3 ft.).

DENNSTAEDTIA

A genus of plants closely allied to and formerly included under the tree ferns. Only one species is known to be reliably hardy.

D. PUNCTILOBULA

(syn. *Dicksonia punctilobula*). Hay-scented Fern. One of my favourite hardy species, and one which should be more widely grown. The graceful lacy fronds are produced in abundance from a thick carpet of twining wiry rhizomes and are covered with minute glands which emit a delightful fragrance of new-mown hay. This is an excellent ground-cover plant which will tolerate any reasonably damp soil in partial shade. Propagation by division of the extensive network of underground stems. (1–3 ft.).

DRYOPTERIS

Male and Buckler Ferns. Almost all the hardy species of *Dryopteris* respond well to cultivation. They are all strong-growing and can withstand most of the indignities a beginner is likely to inflict upon them.

D. AEMULA

Hay-scented Buckler Fern. Graceful native species which derives its common name from the fact that the undersides of the fronds are covered in distinctive stalkless glands which emit a fragrance resembling new-mown hay during warm humid weather, and in the autumn as the fronds start to wither. As this species rarely produces offsets or divisible crowns, spore-raising must be advocated. ($1\frac{1}{2}$–2 ft.).

D. BORRERI

(syn. *D. filix-mas* var. *palacea*). Golden-scaled Male Fern. An exceedingly handsome fern with broad green fronds covered for the entire length of their stalks, or stipes, with distinctive golden scales. It is easily distinguishable from the common Male Fern by the blunted, as opposed to rounded, ends of the pinnules.

Some years ago I wrote an article on the hardy *Dryopteris* species in which I described this plant thus: 'Although of great interest to the botanist and enthusiastic collector, it is doubtful whether this form could hold a place in the heart of the average gardener, who grows plants for his enjoyment and not their botanical intricacies.' At that time I had seen only herbarium (pressed) specimens of the plant which was languishing under the uninspiring name of *D. filix-mas* var. *palacea*. Since then, however, I have come across several plants and now have them well established in my garden, where they are truly a joy to behold. A most commendable plant, which seems to do better in a slightly acid soil. Propagation by spores or division. (2–4 ft.).

D. CARTHUSIANA

(syn. *D. spinulosa*). Narrow or Prickly Buckler Fern. Toothed Woodfern. A fern for moist shady situations where there is a good depth of leafy soil. Its fronds are broadly lance-shaped, two to three feet long, and consist of triangular spined and indented leaflets arranged alternately along the rachis. The sori, or spore-bearing bodies, are borne in two neat rows along the pinnules and erupt during August and September, scattering masses of extremely viable spores, which are capable of bursting into growth in the most inhospitable of situations, and consequently providing a ready means of propagation.

D. DILATATA

(syn. *D. austriaca*). Broad Buckler Fern. A most attractive native which is commonly found growing in the wilds in moist sheltered positions along streamsides and in wet meadows. The fronds are broadly triangular, between two and three feet high, and arise from a stout scaly rootstock. To grow in the garden, plant in a really damp leafy soil. Propagation from spores or by detaching pieces of underground runner each with a terminal cluster of buds. There are several varieties, such as *D. dilatata cristata* and *D. dilatata crispa*, but these are nearly all in private collections and rarely become available to the gardening public.

D. ERYTHROSORA

Although a native of China and Japan, this delightful plant is hardy in most parts of the British Isles. Its triangular fronds are a soft coppery-pink colour when young and contrast markedly with the surrounding green hues of the other *Dryopteris* species. I have not successfully propagated this species, nor have I found a record of methods employed by other gardeners in doing so, but I should imagine from the appearance of the crown that it will eventually divide. I also notice that spores are produced in abundance on the undersides of the fronds, so it will very likely grow from these. ($1\frac{1}{2}$–2 ft.).

Epiphytic, warm-greenhouse,
fern: *Platycerium coronarium*

Moisture-loving, hardy
fern: *Matteuccia struthiopteris*

Epiphytic, warm-greenhouse, fern: *Asplenium nidus*

Moisture-loving fern: *Osmunda regalis*

D. FILIX-MAS

Male Fern. A coarse-growing plant of dignified stature, attaining a height of some three or four feet under favourable conditions. The fronds are lance-shaped and emerge during March from a large woody rootstock. They are often clothed in rust-coloured protective scales, which may persist to a certain degree throughout the summer. Will grow almost anywhere, but prefers moist leafy soil in partial shade. Propagation by spores, although reliable, is extremely slow. Division is a much quicker and practical alternative.

Cultivars or garden forms of *D. filix-mas* are numerous, and exhibit such diverse and complex frond mutations as to be almost totally unrecognizable as belonging to their relatively simple parents. Those which follow I have selected for their attractiveness, ease of cultivation and availability. All can be readily propagated by division.

D. F.-M. BARNESII

An extraordinary variety with long narrow tapering fronds, which are borne in a graceful arching fashion. Will grow absolutely true from spores. (3–4 ft.).

D. F.-M. BOLLANDIAE

Plumose Male Fern. This variety has very finely dissected fronds of a lacy or feathery appearance, which turn to a burnished coppery-red shade at the approach of autumn. (1½–2 ft.).

D. F.-M. CRISTATA

Very similar to the dwarf *D. filix-mas crispa cristata* described in the chapter on rock garden ferns. The leaflets lack the smoothness and lustre exhibited by that variety, and instead of being crimpled and crested are only crested, giving the plant a much more graceful appearance. There are several distinct forms available, two of the most popular being *cristata*

'Jackson', with tall heavily crested fronds reaching a height of some three or four feet, and *cristata* 'Martindale', with decumbent leaflets bending towards the frond tips. Both of these are excellent garden plants and decidedly superior to the more common *cristata*.

D. F.-M. DECOMPOSITA

A handsome broad-fronded form with finely dissected pinnules, or leaflets. (1½–2 ft.).

D. F.-M. GRANDICEPS

The fronds of this plant resemble those of the common Male Fern in texture, colour and stature, but are bedecked at their tips with heavy tassels of crested leaflets. A form known as *D. F.-M.* 'Grandiceps Wills' is sometimes grown, and can be easily distinguished by the enormous much branched crests, which weigh heavily on the tall resplendent fronds. (2–4 ft.).

D. GOLDIANA

Goldie Fern, Giant Woodfern. A handsome north-east American native which may attain a height of four or five feet under favourable conditions. Its enormous grey-green fronds are held aloft on long scaly stipes, or stalks, and are broadly spear-shaped in outline. Spores are borne in abundance beneath the fronds, but I have found that they seldom germinate under artificial conditions, and consequently propagation by division must be advocated.

D. MARGINALIS

Marginal Shield Fern. Marginal Buckler Fern, Leather Woodfern. This North American species is a most accommodating plant, superficially looking very much like a refined Male Fern (*D. filix-mas*), and enjoying much the same kind of growing conditions. Its fronds are between eighteen inches and two feet long, lance-shaped, and grow from a stout tufted rootstock. A variety known as *D. marginalis* var. *elegans* is identical to the species, except for the pinnules, or leaflets, which are enlarged to approximately twice the size. Propagation is by spores or division of the crowns in autumn.

D. WALLICHIANA

A very choice and rare fern. In spring the young fronds are bright yellowish-green with contrasting black stems. These eventually turn green and then look more like those of *D. borreri*. Division is the only satisfactory method of propagation, but this is very slow.

LYGODIUM

Climbing Ferns. These ferns offer a complete contrast to the more normal terrestrial species, embracing some forty or so species, which are distributed throughout the tropical and sub-tropical regions of all continents, and characterized by a twining rachis, unique amongst the pteridophytes.

L. PALMATUM

An eastern North American species, and the only one which can be planted outside with any safety. But even this plant appreciates a light covering of straw or bracken during the winter months until well established. The quaint heart-shaped leaflets are liberally produced along thin wiry stems, which during a good season will grow to a length of some four or six feet and quickly festoon any bush within reach. Propagation is by spores, which are produced in abundance on curious little catkin-like fructifications during early autumn.

OSMUNDA

Royal Ferns. The distinguished title of 'royal' has long been conferred upon this splendid group of plants, but it has now come to refer more specifically to *O. regalis*, which is dealt with in the chapter on moisture-loving ferns. All the *Osmundas* are bulky plants with large fibrous rootstocks, which yield the osmunda fibre that is used so extensively in orchid composts.

O. CINNAMOMEA

Cinnamon Fern. The coppery coloured woolly growth which covers the young fronds as they emerge in the spring is one of the most striking characteristics of this species. Unfortunately this disappears long before the imposing soft green fronds have completely unfurled, but is replaced by another important feature; indeed the one to which the plant's common name alludes. In the midst of the abundant green barren fronds an occasional fertile one appears. This is stout and erect, and covered with an extensive terminal cluster of cinnamon-coloured spore-bearing bodies which gives the fruiting portion a distinctive mottled appearance. For the best results plant this species in a rich moist leafy soil in woodland or semi-shaded conditions. Propagation by spores sown as soon as they ripen is the best method. Divisions occasionally fail to take, and even those that do, tend to grow one-sided for several years, unless of course you are fortunate enough to find a double- or treble-'nosed' plant. (3–5 ft.).

O. CLAYTONIANA

Interrupted Fern. This is the most extraordinary member of the genus, deriving its common name from the fact that the spores are borne in a solid mass around the stipe, or stalk, in a central area of the frond which is completely devoid of leafy pinnæ. The leaflets above and below this fructification are quite normally developed, giving the entire frond the appearance of having been interrupted. The surrounding green sterile fronds are quite normal and of a soft velvety texture, making a perfect contrast for the chocolate brown sori. Plant in a cool moist position in partial shade. Propagation is by spores sown immediately after ripening. (3 ft.).

PHYLLITIS

Hart's Tongue Ferns. Tough, easily grown ferns with broad, solid fronds which resemble Dock leaves rather than fern fronds. Most will grow in either dry or damp conditions in full sun or dense shade.

P. SCOLOPENDRIUM

(syn. *Scolopendrium vulgare*). Hart's Tongue Fern. A frequent inhabitant of woodland, hedgerow and open ground throughout Wales, northern and western England and southern Scotland, especially on slightly alkaline soils. The solid leaf blade is bright green, leathery, and carries distinctive rows of sori on the reverse. These it was once thought looked like centipedes, and it was from this that the old-fashioned name of Scolopendrium (Scolopendra—a centipede) was derived. Propagation by spores, division or frond bases. (1½–2½ ft.).

Many varieties of the Hart's Tongue Fern have been evolved over the years but very few have remained in cultivation. Those which are listed are some of the most striking and readily available. (see also Rock Garden Ferns).

P. S. CAPITATUM

The fronds of this variety are normal except for a heavy terminal crest. (9 in.–1½ ft.).

P. S. DIGITATUM

A very fine form of *cristatus* origin, with flat branching crests that are spread out like a hand. (9 in.–1½ ft.).

P. S. LACERATUM

Curious fronds that are indented along their margins, thereby creating an irregular lobed appearance. (9 in.–1½ ft.).

POLYSTICHUM

Shield Ferns. Common inhabitants of hedgerows and woodlands throughout the temperate regions of the world. Known as Shield Ferns on account of the round shield-like indusia which cover and protect the sori.

P. ACHROSTICHOIDES

Holly Fern. A handsome fern from North America which is completely evergreen and garnered in great quantities from its

natural haunts for decoration during the festive season. The
dark-green fronds are lance-shaped, coarse-growing and of a
glossy and leathery texture. In spring the emerging fronds are
covered in glistening white felty scales, but these disappear
completely as the summer wears on. An excellent subject for
any soil in a partially shaded position. Propagation by spores
or division. (1–2½ ft.).

P. ACULEATUM

Hard Shield Fern. The broad lance-shaped fronds of this
fern are arranged in a circular fashion around a short woody
rootstock. They are dark green and leathery above, grey-green
and soft beneath, and carry neat rows of sori on the undersides
of the leaflets. The stalks, or stipes, are densely clothed in rust-
coloured scales. A form known as *P. aculeatum* var. *lobatum*
has narrow fronds and much larger and coarser leaflets. Both
seem to do well anywhere where there are liberal amounts of
water available. Propagation by spores or division of the
crowns in autumn. (1–2½ ft.).

P. MUNITUM

American Sword Fern. Very similar to *P. achrostichoides*
but decidedly inferior. Formerly grown quite extensively, but
nowadays seldom encountered in gardens. The fronds are long,
narrow and quite prickly. Propagation by spores or division.
(1–1½ ft.).

P. SETIFERUM

(syn. *P. angulare*). Soft Shield Fern. A very closely related
species to *P. aculeatum* and formerly described as a variety of
the same. The fronds are pale green and much less crowded
than those of *P. aculeatum*, but otherwise identical. The rootstock is hard and woody, and covered with large brown scales
which extend right up the stipes, or frond stalks. These are
quite flexible and no doubt account to a certain extent for the
plant's common name of soft shield fern. An easily cultivated

plant in moist shady positions. Propagation by spores or division. (1–2½ ft.).

Apart from being a most desirable acquisition in itself, *P. setiferum* has also given rise to many fine garden varieties with tassellated and much divided fronds.

P. S. CRISTOGRACILE MOLY

Erect crested pea-green fronds with pinnules that terminate in a membraneous projection. (1–1½ ft.).

P. S. DIVISILOBUM

Probably the most popular form of *P. setiferum*. The broad fronds consist of a multitude of finely cut leaflets which divide at the ends into pointed finger-like projections. The fronds grow to about two feet high, are dark green, and supported on short, extremely hairy and scaly stipes, or frond stalks. Two forms known as 'Divisilobum Densum' and 'D.D. Superbum' respectively, are decidedly superior to the above but do not appear to be as robust or long-lived.

P. S. MANICA-INFANTIS

Tall, narrow fronds with pinnules that are reminiscent of a small child's hand. (1–2½ ft.).

P. S. PLUMOSO-DIVISILOBUM

Dense finely cut fronds which take on a soft mossy appearance. Very beautiful and highly recommended. (1–2½ ft.).

P. S. PULCHERRIMUM

An exceedingly fine fern with graceful feathery fronds arranged around a central core of stem. To enjoy the full beauty of this plant it is imperative to restrict it to a single crown. Therefore all young stock that appears around the base should be removed each year. This will form a ready means of propagation and at the same time ensure that the parent does not lose its attractive symmetry. (1–2 ft.).

THELYPTERIS

A comparatively new classification which embraces several popular ferns formerly known as *Dryopteris*, *Phegopteris* and *Polypodium*.

T. PHEGOPTERIS

(syn. *Dryopteris phegopteris*, *Polypodium phegopteris*, *Phegopteris polypodioides*). Beech Fern. A quaint little plant for carpeting beneath trees or clothing a shady pocket on the rock garden. The fronds arise singly from a creeping mat of rhizomes and consist of numerous tiny triangular leaflets supported on wiry stems. It is a fern which seems to do much better in an acid soil in a position where its rootstock can creep undisturbed and with little competition from other plants. Propagation by spores or division of the creeping underground stems. (9 in.–1 ft.).

6

Moisture-loving Ferns

Many gardeners have a damp area of ground in close proximity to their ornamental pool, or a part of the flower border, which is permanently wet and totally unsuitable for accommodating the popular kinds of showy herbaceous perennials and bedding plants. But such a position is ideal for the cultivation of various species of moisture-loving ferns, either alone, or as a soft green foil to the reds, yellows and oranges of the bog garden Primulas, Hostas and Trollius. To be really successful with these subjects, it is essential to incorporate liberal quantities of coarse peat into the soil before planting, as this not only helps to retain moisture but provides a degree of acidity, which these species appreciate.

DRYOPTERIS CRISTATA

Crested Buckler Fern. A native of wet marshy ground which will readily establish itself in the bog garden or by the pool side. When its scaly creeping rhizomes are allowed to colonize the moist low-lying areas they will thrust up sturdy pale green fronds in abundance. As the fronds unfurl they reveal a most interesting characteristic which enables one to identify the species whilst it is still in an immature state. The pinnæ, or leaflets, expand rapidly below the uncoiling frond tip and appear to embrace it. It grows best in a slightly acid soil. Propagation is by division of the rhizomes. (1 ft.).

MATTEUCIA STRUTHIOPTERIS

(syn. *Struthiopteris germanica*). Ostrich Feather Fern. Handsome pea-green fronds arranged in a shuttlecock fashion around a stout woody rootstock. The fertile fronds are about half the length of the barren ones and produced from the centre of the 'shuttlecock' during mid-summer. This tough and resilient species spreads rapidly by means of wiry underground runners. (3–5 ft.).

ONOCLEA SENSIBILIS

Sensitive Fern. A splendid waterside fern with erect flattened fronds that arise from a thick black creeping rhizome. On unfurling they are an attractive rose-pink colour but change rapidly as the summer progresses to an agreeable shade of pale green. This species enjoys really wet conditions and a soil rich in humus, and is never happier than when planted close to a pool where its spreading rhizomes can creep into the water and colonize the shallower areas. (1½–2 ft.).

OSMUNDA REGALIS

Royal Fern. A tall and stately fern with large leathery fronds which vary between four and six feet in height, and change colour with age from pale lime-green to rich burnished bronze. Unfortunately their glowing autumnal tints are short-lived, for the foliage is very tender, and at the first touch of frost shrivels and hangs limply from the woody semi-persistent frond stalks. Although it is completely hardy it is advisable to cover the over-wintering crowns with a thick layer of straw or bracken to give some measure of protection to the emerging young fronds.

Propagation is easily effected from spores, which are produced on the fertile fronds in extensive terminal clusters during May and June. These should be sown immediately after gathering, for unlike the majority of other fern species, each spore of the Osmunda contains a small quantity of chlorophyll which renders it viable only for two or three days.

In addition to the true species there are three varieties which are worthy of special mention. The Crested Royal Fern (*O. regalis* 'Cristata'), a most desirable plant with fronds that terminate in attractive tassels of twisted leaflets; *Osmunda regalis* 'Undulata', with crimpled and crested fronds, and the purple-leafed variety, *Osmunda regalis* 'Purpurescens'.

THELYPTERIS PALUSTRIS

(syn. *Dryopteris thelypteris*). Marsh Buckler Fern. An extremely elegant fern with finely cut fronds, which are produced singly at irregular intervals from a creeping mat of black wiry roots. Both barren and fertile fronds are usually in evidence, the latter often persisting well into the winter. (2–3 ft.).

WOODWARDIA VIRGINICA

Virginian Chain Fern. Very similar in growth to *Onoclea sensibilis*. Broad, olive-green fronds of a soft felty texture are produced from a stout creeping rootstock. Difficulty may be experienced initially in establishing this species, for it often takes a whole season before starting active growth, and during this waiting period the unwary gardener can do untold damage by poking and prying in the area of the dormant root. But once this dormancy is broken there is no containing the plant, the thick black knotted rootstocks spreading rapidly in all directions much in the same manner as those of the common Bracken. (1½–2½ ft.).

7

Rock Garden Ferns

Many species of ferns make excellent and most accommodating subjects for the rock garden, rapidly clothing vacant pockets and providing a refreshing green foil for their more gaudy alpine neighbours. There are numerous varieties of dwarf habit from which to choose, but the beginner would be wise to concentrate his efforts on varieties of *Asplenium, Polypodium, Cystopteris* and the dwarf forms of *Dryopteris* and *Athyrium*.

ADIANTUM

Maidenhair Ferns. Only three species of Adiantum are capable of withstanding the rigours of a British winter in the open. All of these are comparatively easy-going, asking only for a cool moist acid soil and a total lack of deep cultivation in the immediate vicinity of their roots. Propagation is easily effected by dividing up the black scaly creeping rhizomes, which should then be potted and stood in a cold frame until they become well established.

A. JAPONICUM

Rose-Fronded Maidenhair. An exquisite little fern capable of bestowing its oriental charm on the dullest and darkest of corners. The dainty, almost pendant, fronds emerge during April and are a pleasant shade of rose-pink. As the summer progresses, however, these change through bronze to soft green. (1–1½ ft.).

A. PEDATUM

Hardy Maidenhair. This delightful North American species

is probably the commonest hardy *Adiantum*. Its two-foot-high
fronds consist of long glistening black wiry stalks which
support legions of delicate pale green, kidney-shaped leaflets.
A dwarf variety known variously as *A. pedatum* 'Klondike'
and *A. pedatum* var. *aleuticum* is often grown and has proved to
be much more reliable in exposed situations.

A. VENUSTUM

Kashmir Maidenhair. Dwarf, very leafy fronds which change
colour with age from soft green with a metallic sheen to golden-
yellow, and finally reddish-brown after the first severe frost.
The dead fronds remain in character throughout the winter,
their dried-up leaflets clinging to the old stalks in much the
same manner as beech foliage clings to a beech hedge.
(6 in.–1 ft.).

ASPLENIUM

Spleenworts. Charming little ferns which will grow satisfactorily in crevices and niches between rocks as well as on the
open rock garden. There are quite a number of different hardy
varieties known to botanists, but only a few respond really well
to cultivation. All resent disturbance of the roots and well-
meaning attempts at division, but will propagate quite readily
from spores.

A. ADIANTUM-NIGRUM

Black Spleenwort. Attractive almost triangular fresh green
fronds held aloft on slender shiny black frond stalks. Easily
grown in a stony soil in partial shade. (6–9 in.).

A. PLATYNEURON

Ebony Spleenwort. A North American species requiring
similar growing conditions to the Black Spleenwort. Its fronds
are long and narrow, with conspicuous black stems, and rather
like enlarged and superior versions of those of the common
Maidenhair Spleenwort. (1½–2 ft.).

A. RUTA-MURARIA

Wall Rue. The smallest of the Spleenworts. Tiny stiff, almost evergreen, wedge-shaped fronds arise from a short scaleless rootstock. In its wild state, this plant is found growing in rock crevices amongst mosses and lichens; conditions which are difficult to simulate in a garden, except possibly in a dry wall. Great success can be achieved, however, by growing this species in a mixture of equal parts loam and peat in the holes of a common house air-brick; the brick being stood on edge so that the plants can cascade down its face. (1–3 in.).

A. TRICHOMANES

Maidenhair Spleenwort. This is undoubtedly the best known and most popular species. Slender arching fronds some six to eight inches in length support legions of round dull green leaflets, which fall off at the approach of winter, leaving the old shiny black frond stalks naked. Little trouble should be experienced in growing this small fern if given a cool position on the rock garden in a well-drained calcareous soil.

A. VIRIDE

Green Spleenwort. Very similar to the preceding species and for many years thought to be merely a variety of the same. The fronds have attractive green stems and are of a flaccid nature. Cultural requirements are the same as recommended for the Maidenhair Spleenwort. (6–8 in.).

ATHYRIUM

Lady Ferns. Several small varieties of our popular Lady Fern are suitable for rock garden cultivation. They like moist peaty soil in a partially shaded location.

A. DISTENTIFOLIUM

(syn. *A. alpestre*). Alpine Lady Fern. A comparatively rare native of very similar appearance to the common Lady Fern.

Its soft lance-shaped fronds are pale green, and arise in a circle from a short scaly rootstock. ($1\frac{1}{2}$–$2\frac{1}{2}$ ft.).

A. FILIX-FEMINA

Lady Fern. Although the bulk of varieties of this species are woodland plants and have been dealt with in an earlier chapter, there are several diminutive forms suitable for the rock garden or alpine house.

A. F.-F. CONGESTUM

This is a very variable form, with dwarf congested fronds no more than eight inches high. Although good plants can be raised from spores it is advisable to propagate choice variants by division.

A. F.-F. CRISPUM

An unusual little fern with crisp, slightly crested fronds, growing from a thickly matted rootstock. (4–5 in.).

A. F.-F. FRIZELLIAE CRISTATUM

An exceptionally fine crested form of the Tatting Fern. Each frond is almost weighed down to the ground by its extensive terminal crest. (9 in.–1 ft.).

A. F.-F. MINUTISSIMA

Dainty Lady Fern. Dainty pale lime green fronds rarely more than six inches high, which are complete miniature replicas of those of *A. filix-femina*. Propagation presents no problems, for this little fern spreads rapidly by strong black wiry rhizomes and throws up easily divisible clumps of fronds at regular intervals.

BLECHNUM

Splendid evergreen ferns for a lime-free soil. Unfortunately very few species are reliably hardy, only one alpine kind growing happily outside in Britain.

B. PENNA-MARINA

Both barren and fertile fronds of this species are very distinct and handsome. The former are dark green, leathery, and rarely exceed six inches in length, whereas the spore-bearing ones stand erect in the centre of the plant and are quite nine inches to a foot high. Under favourable conditions this species forms an attractive dark green carpet.

CAMPTOSORUS RHIZOPHYLLUS

Walking Fern. A charming little fern which produces successions of shiny heart-shaped fronds in a manner which suggests steps. These often root at their tips and occasionally produce plantlets from them. The individual fronds are between six and nine inches long, lance shaped, and borne on naked reddish frond stalks. Although not one of the easiest species to grow, reasonable success can be assured by planting in a dry shady pocket and protecting from excessive dampness during winter. (6–9 in.).

CETERACH OFFICINARUM

Rusty Back Fern. An easy-going native with narrow lance-shaped leathery fronds, the reverses covered in a dense layer of brown chaffy scales. These fronds are curious in that in times of drought the leaflets roll inwards and the plant will appear to be quite dead, but after a shower of rain these will expand again and assume their old positions. Almost any gritty soil in a well-drained open position will support this plant happily. (6–9 in.).

CRYPTOGRAMMA CRISPA

(syn. *Allosorus crispa*). Parsley Fern. As its common name implies, this fern may be likened to parsley, but I always think this comparison a little unkind, for the fronds are like verdant

Shade-loving ferns: *Blechnum spicant*

Athyrium filix-femina plumosum

Moisture-loving *Thelypteris palustris* growing in marsh

filigree and are borne with an air of grace and elegance that even a Maidenhair would be hard pressed to emulate. A frequent inhabitant of the mountainous regions of Scotland, this little plant is a fanatical lime-hater and should not be attempted where there is any hint of alkalinity in the soil. (6–9 in.).

CYSTOPTERIS

Bladder Ferns. These are without doubt the finest group of ferns for rock garden and alpine house culture. They all possess graceful lacy fronds that are of a delicate membraneous nature, a characteristic which is usually associated only with the filmy ferns. On the undersides of the fronds are scattered the dark brown sori, or spore-bearing bodies, each protected by a blister-like structure which doubtless inspired early botanists to refer to them as Bladder Ferns. All species are deciduous, losing their fronds completely at the first touch of frost.

C. ALPINA

Alpine Bladder Fern. Very similar to our native *C. fragilis*, differing only in the divisions and venation of the frond. (9 in.).

C. BULBIFERA

Berry Bladder Fern. This North American native looks superficially like a larger version of *C. fragilis* with weak stems. Because of this characteristic it is usually thought advisable to place a small framework of twiggy material around the crown in early spring, so that the emerging fronds can grow through and obtain support from the temporary structure. Propagation is easily affected by collecting the tiny bulbils which form in rows beneath the fronds, and treating them like seedlings. (1½–2 ft.).

C. DICKIEANA

Arctic Bladder Fern. Tiny fronds seldom exceeding three inches in height, with rather coarse lobed and notched leaflets which overlap one another, and to a certain extent destroy the beautiful filigree effect so admirably created by the other species. This little fern is extremely rare, and as far as I am aware occurs only in the wild in sheltered coastal districts in very limited areas of Scotland. Therefore, if one is fortunate enough to secure a specimen, it is best to assign it to the alpine house, where it can receive the special attention it merits. I find it grows best in a well-drained earthenware pan, with a compost of equal parts peat, loam and non-calcareous sandstone which is kept just moist by a daily overhead spraying of soft water.

C. FRAGILIS

Brittle Bladder Fern. A most charming and endearing plant, with fragile, broadly lance-shaped, translucent fronds. These are about nine inches high and arise from a prostrate rootstock, which is thickly covered in broad golden-brown scales. Although spores are freely produced, they are seldom used for propagation because the rootstocks are readily divisible. Apart from the species, there is the Crested Brittle Bladder Fern, *C. fragilis cristata*, a mutant with quaintly crested leaflets. This is a real gem, which needs growing in an alpine house if one is to do it justice.

C. MONTANA

Mountain Bladder Fern. A most distinctive plant, with short triangular pale green fronds which are produced individually from a creeping black rootstock. I have always found propagation by spores very unreliable with this species, and division a far better proposition. The short pieces of black root are potted in a compost of equal parts peat, loam and pea-shingle, and stood in a cold frame until established. (8 in.–1 ft.).

DRYOPTERIS

Male and Buckler Ferns. Tough, yet accommodating plants, usually associated with moist woodland areas. All the smaller varieties become readily established on the rock garden and provide a splendid contrast to their colourful alpine neighbours.

D. ASSIMILIS

(syn. *D. dilatata alpina*). A small variety of local occurrence in mountainous regions of the British Isles. Looks very much like a dwarf form of *D. dilatata*, with delicate, light green fronds. Enjoys partial shade in a good free-draining loam. (6–9 in.).

D. BORRERI CONGESTA CRISTATA

Very dwarf form of the Golden Scaled Male Fern, with congested fronds that are attractively crested. (6–9 in.).

D. FILIX-MAS

Several varieties of the common Male Fern respond well to rock garden treatment.

D. F.-M. CRISPA CRISTATA

Heavily crested and crimpled fronds, which are uncharacteristically smooth and shiny, and of an exceptionally deep pea-green colour. On the rock garden this variety soon forms spreading clumps which divide easily for propagation purposes. (1–1½ ft.).

D. F.-M. LINEARIS CONGESTA

A compact plant with finely divided fronds. (6–9 in.).

D. F.-M. POLYDACTYLA

Short narrow fronds which rarely exceed eighteen inches in height. The tips are divided into very brittle finger-like crests which, instead of taking a typical pendant poise, remain stiffly straight and erect. In well-grown plants the fronds are dark olive-green, but seem only to attain this colour when pot-grown. For some unaccountable reason open ground plants develop a type of chlorosis, which shows as a fine green mottling on a pale yellow background. The plants do not seem to suffer unduly from this disorder, but nevertheless look decidedly sick when seen intermingled with the bright green foliage of the other hardy *Dryopteris* species.

D. HEXAGONOPTERA

Winged Woodfern. A diminutive native of north-eastern U.S.A. with frail triangular fronds barely nine inches high. They arise from a wiry black creeping rhizome, and are carried on slender but persistent straw-coloured stems.

D. VILLARSII

Rigid Buckler Fern. An extremely tough fern which is found in its wild state growing out of rock fissures in elevated limestone regions. Its fronds are upright, deeply cut, and arise from a coarse scaly rootstock. (1–1½ ft.).

GYMNOCARPIUM DRYOPTERIS

(syn. *Thelypteris dryopteris*). Oak Fern. Soft yellowish-green fronds some nine inches high are produced from a slender underground creeping stem which delights in wandering amongst stony soil on a shaded part of the rock garden. A variety of this, *G. dryopteris plumosum*, is even more beautiful.

G. ROBERTIANUM

(syn. *Thelypteris robertianum*). Limestone Polypody. Very similar in appearance to the Oak Fern, but perhaps a little smaller. Its black rhizome, which is covered in brown scales and golden hairs, will form a dense carpet in any vacant pocket on the rockery. (6–9 in.).

PELLAEA ATROPURPUREA

Purple Cliff Brake. An outstanding North American native

which has adapted itself well to cultivation. The fronds are very delicate, lance-shaped, and have conspicuous purplish-black stems. This little fern does best in full sun in a well-drained alkaline soil. Propagation by spores is most reliable, literally hundreds of young plants being raised from a single sowing. (6 in.–1 ft.).

PHYLLITIS SCOLOPENDRIUM

(syn. *Scolopendrium vulgare*). Hart's Tongue Fern. Most of the varietal forms of our native Hart's Tongue Fern are small and compact enough to be comfortably accommodated on the average rock garden. Those mentioned below are a selection of the kinds most useful in this situation.

P. S. CRISPUM

An exceedingly fine form with frond margins that are crinkled and frilled. Several variations are available, none of which come true from spores, so division has to be relied upon for propagation purposes. (9 in.–1½ ft.).

P. S. CRISTATUM

A smaller version of the common species with an attractive fan-like crest. (9 in.–1½ ft.).

P. S. RAMO-CRISTATUM

The fronds of this variety branch into flat terminal crests. Forms of this type are not infrequently seen growing wild in the Welsh mountains. (9 in.–1½ ft.).

P. S. SAGITTATUM

A medium growing plant with arrow-shaped fronds of the deepest green. (9 in.–1½ ft.).

POLYPODIUM VULGARE

Common Polypody. A familiar native which is adaptable to almost any conditions. Short sharply cut lance-shaped evergreen fronds arise from a yellowish creeping rhizome that is densely clothed in reddish-brown scales. Much confusion exists as to what exactly constitutes the typical species, but this is generally only of interest to the botanist who is delving into chromosomes and genetics to establish various taxonomic facts, and has no direct bearing on the garden merit of the plant. Division of the rhizome is the best method of propagation, although the plant will grow reasonably well from spores. (3 in.–1 ft.).

P. V. BIFIDUM

Almost identical to the preceding, except that the lower pinnae or leaflets are divided into two at their tips. (6 in.–1 ft.).

P. V. CAMBRICUM

An unusual plant originally discovered growing wild in Wales. The fronds are distinctly toothed towards the edges and of a much thinner texture than the common species. Propagation by division. (6 in.–1 ft.).

P. V. CORNUBIENSE

An extraordinary fern with three distinct types of frond; the normal *P. vulgare* type, very finely divided ones, and a number which are intermediate between the two. The common kind of frond should always be removed as soon as it becomes evident, or the more desirable portion of the plant will be overwhelmed. (6 in.).

P. V. CRISTATUM

Attractive cristate variety with semi-pendulous terminal crests. Several selected and much improved forms are in cultivation. (6 in.–1 ft.).

P. V. RAMOSUM

At first glance this seems to be identical with the common species but closer inspection will reveal that the fronds branch repeatedly from the base. (6 in.–1 ft.).

POLYSTICHUM

Shield Ferns. A few varieties of these popular ferns respond quite well to rock garden culture. *Polystichum lonchitis* is the only true mountain or rock garden species.

P. LONCHITIS

Holly Fern. Evergreen spear-shaped fronds with sharply toothed leaflets are the characteristics that have earned this plant the popular name of Holly Fern. Being a native of stony haunts in Snowdonia and the Scottish Highlands, this little fern appreciates a good gritty loam in a position that is not too exposed to drying winds or the effects of prolonged sunshine. Grows very readily from spores. A variety which I must confess I have never seen, *P. lonchitis* var. *bulbiferum*, apparently produces small bulbils from the bases of the lower pinnae, or leaflets. (6–9 in.).

P. PROLIFERUM

A most delightful little fern, possibly a variety of our native *P. setiferum*, with finely divided broadly lance-shaped fronds which bear rows of young plants along the central ribs of the fronds. The fronds are almost evergreen, persisting in a bronze-green state until long after the fresh young ones have emerged. (6 in.–1 ft.).

P. SETIFERUM

Soft Shield Fern. As mentioned in an earlier chapter, this species has given rise to a superabundance of choice garden forms. Some of the more diminutive kinds make excellent rock garden subjects.

P. S. CONGESTUM

Small congested fronds in which the individual pinnae overlap one another. Two crested forms, *P. setiferum congestum cristatum* and *P. setiferum congestum grandiceps* are fairly frequently encountered. (6 in.).

P. S. CRISTATUM

Many different crested forms are in cultivation and usually classified under this general heading. One exception, however, is *P. setiferum cristatum* 'Wollaston', with a heavy terminal crest. All do well in a free-draining soil which is rich in humus and in a partially shaded situation. (6 in.–1½ ft.).

P. S. POLYDACTYLUM

A curious variety in which the pinnae, or leaflets, have extended finger-like crests. (9 in.–1½ ft.).

WOODSIA

These are alpine ferns of little garden merit, but often grown by very keen gardeners. The plants are easily satisfied with a coarse gritty soil in an open pocket on the rock garden. Two species, *W. ilvensis* and *W. alpina* are native, and the ones that are usually grown. (3–6 in.).

8

Cool-greenhouse Ferns

The cool greenhouse is extremely useful for fern culture, for here many of the hardy varieties can be grown to perfection alongside some of their more exotic, slightly tender counterparts. A cool greenhouse, for the purposes of this book, may be taken to be one in which artificial heat is not normally given, except in the depths of winter, and then only to keep the frost at bay. All the plants suggested in this chapter adapt well to culture in the living-room when provided with ample moisture and a shady corner.

ADIANTUM

Maidenhair Ferns. Although many of these graceful ferns will grow in a cool greenhouse with some effect, it is only when in a warmer environment that they really come into their own. Most varieties have very delicate and sensitive fronds and should not be exposed to strong sunlight in the early stages of growth. Mature plants can be acclimatized to more intense light by moving the pots around the house every few weeks, bringing them a little closer to the glass each time. In this way the plants have their foliage hardened without loss of colour, which in turn makes them more adaptable for general decorative purposes.

All *Adiantums* appreciate a lumpy loam compost with a little charcoal added to keep it sweet. They like to grow in a moist, well-drained medium and will not on any account tolerate stagnant soil. Propagation is easily affected by spores, although in some cases careful division may be possible.

A. CAPILLUS-VENERIS

A native species occasionally encountered in the wild,

growing in damp shady rock crevices in sheltered coastal areas. Despite being an indigenous plant, its fronds are often cut back by early frosts, so it is better to keep it confined to the greenhouse. Plants that are grown outside always look very tatty and sorry for themselves. The fronds are more or less evergreen and arise from a tough wiry rootstock. The leafy portion of the frond is triangular, with bluish-green pinnae, or leaflets, alternately placed along shiny black stipes and rachis. Spores are produced in abundance along the margins of the leaflets, which fold over to give them protection in typical *Adiantum* fashion. More than twenty different varieties of this were in cultivation before the turn of the century, but it is doubtful whether any remain, other than in private hands. (6 in.–2 ft.).

A. HISPIDULUM

Like an enlarged version of the hardy *A. pedatum*, but with young fronds that are a delightful shade of rose-pink on emerging during early spring. An adaptable plant that will grow in a sunnier position than most other species. (9 in.–2 ft.).

ASPLENIUM

Spleenworts. The cool house species are easily grown and very adaptable, doing well in John Innes compost No. 2 with a little grit added. All will grow from spores with a varying degree of success.

A. BULBIFERUM

Mother Spleenwort. One of the easiest and most rewarding ferns for a beginner to try. A little gem, with finely divided dark green fronds along which develop bulbils that produce little fronds. If a leaf bearing these is pegged down to a pan of compost, these bulbils will root and form new plants. (6 in.–1 ft.).

A. FALCATUM

A handsome New Zealand native with arching lance-shaped dark green fronds with dull green undersides. Some gardeners consider planting this fern outside to be a calculated risk, but I have found that it seldom does well, and prefer to keep it in a frost-free greenhouse. (1–1½ ft.).

A. FLABELLIFOLIUM

Necklace Fern. This is a useful fern for both pot and basket work. The pendant fronds are long and narrow with widely separated leaflets, which gives them a necklace-like appearance. Allow plenty of space between plants so that air can circulate freely. (6 in.–1 ft.).

A. FLACCIDUM

Hanging Spleenwort. This is an unusual species which may be encountered from time to time. It is basically epiphytic and prefers a well-drained compost consisting of approximately one part loam, two parts grit, and three parts peat. I find it very useful as a basket plant, for its pale green leathery fronds are pendant and may be anything up to three feet long.

BLECHNUM

Some of the species which are on the borderline of hardiness can be grown to advantage even in a totally unheated greenhouse. Always use a lime-free compost, which should otherwise be based on the John Innes No. 2 formula. Propagation is by spores, although occasionally easily detachable young plants are produced around the crowns.

B. CAPENSE

Palm Leaf Fern. A variable species from New Zealand with lance-shaped barren fronds which may attain a height of four feet under favourable conditions. The fertile fronds are typically erect, carry dense terminal fructification, and are usually a few inches taller than the barren ones.

B. DISCOLOR

Glossy green leathery fronds with greyish or sometimes

brownish undersides are the great attraction of this plant. The young fronds are also a deep coppery colour as they emerge during early spring. In my opinion this is the best of the cultivated Blechnum species. (1–3 ft.).

CHEILANTHES

Lip Ferns. A group of ferns around which much controversy lies as regards naming. They are quite closely related to the *Adiantums* and are equally decorative. Most species appreciate a quick-draining compost, which should be basically like that prescribed for *Adiantums* but with a little grit added. Always grow in a well-ventilated house and water carefully. Propagation is by spores and sometimes by division.

C. DISTANS

A small bushy plant with dark green somewhat hairy triangular fronds. Grow in a sunny position quite close to the glass. (3–9 in.).

C. FRAGRANS

It is a shame that this fern is not more widely known for it is truly a plantsman's delight. The small dark green fronds are slightly hairy beneath and emit a fragrance of freshly gathered violets. Plant in the normal compost but with a handful of peat mixed in for each plant to be potted. (3–9 in.).

C. LANOSA

Although usually regarded as completely hardy, I always find that this little species appreciates the protection of a cold greenhouse or frame. Its fronds are triangular or sometimes lance-shaped with hairy black stalks, or stipes, which in turn carry soft green foliage that is densely covered in whitish silky hairs. Be sure to add plenty of grit to the compost and avoid splashing water on the foliage. (6–9 in.).

C. MARANTAE

Probably the most uninspiring member of the family, but one which I consider worth growing solely for the striking chestnut-coloured scales that densely clothe the lower portions of the fronds. Sometimes grown outdoors on the rock garden in mild districts. (6–8 in.).

CYATHEA

A large family of tree ferns, many of which get too big for the average greenhouse. Several species are worth consideration, for they are easily grown and may take up to twenty years before attaining unmanageable proportions. I like to use John Innes compost No. 3 with a handful of well-rotted manure or old leaves mixed in near the bottom of the pot. Propagation is almost exclusively by spores.

C. COLENSOI

Probably the toughest species but unfortunately quite difficult to come by. The trunk is semi-prostrate, only a couple of inches thick, and has long yellowish-green or bronze green fronds which are clothed in persistent hairs and scales. Owing to its sprawling nature it is best accommodated in the greenhouse border when such is available. (2–4 ft.).

C. CUNNINGHAMII

Gully Tree Fern. Very similar in general appearance to *C. medullaris* but with a smaller trunk and more dainty fronds. In New Zealand the trunks are often cut for use as fence posts. (Up to 12 ft.).

C. DEALBATA

Silver Tree Fern. Large spreading soft green fronds with silvery undersides. Requires considerable shade before giving of its best. (Up to 10 ft.).

C. MEDULLARIS

Black Tree Fern. Undoubtedly the largest and fastest growing New Zealand species. The expansive fronds are rich green, with coarse hairy stipes and produced in abundance from a stout black trunk. It soon outgrows its allocated space but creates a splendid effect when young. (Up to 20 ft.).

C. SMITHII

Soft Tree Fern. An elegant moisture-loving species with fresh green fronds borne horizontally from the trunk. A useful and resilient little plant. (Up to 8 ft.).

CYRTOMIUM

Handsome ferns of easy culture and of great value because of the evergreen nature of their fronds. John Innes compost No. 2 makes an admirable medium for them when enriched with a little well-rotted manure. Propagation is by spores or division.

C. FALCATUM

Holly Fern. Produces masses of glossy fronds with large holly-like leaflets that remain in character throughout the year. The emerging fronds are sometimes covered in whitish or brown scales, which provide an added attraction. (1–2 ft.).

C. F. ROCHFORDII

A splendid selection which is a little more compact than the preceding but otherwise very similar. (1–2 ft.).

DAVALLIA

Hare's-foot Fern. Ferns which are more usually associated with the warm greenhouse, yet which provide a couple of species for the less fortunate gardener with only cool house conditions. They are really epiphytic plants, but under cultivation seem to respond well to being grown in pans of leafy or peaty compost, across which their substantial creeping rhizomes can travel. It is these rhizomes which have given rise to their being called Hare's-foot Ferns, for they are covered in brownish hairy scales, giving them the resemblance of an animal's foot. All species are deciduous and require a short dormant drying-off period in the winter. Propagation is by spores or occasionally division.

D. MARIESII

Supposedly the hardiest species, but I feel it is a trifle risky to try it outdoors in our temperamental climate. The fronds are dark olive-green, roughly triangular, and produced at intervals from the thick creeping rhizome. An easily grown plant under cool greenhouse conditions. (6 in.–1 ft.).

D. TRICHOMANOIDES

(syn. *D. dissecta*). A variable species with short triangular or lance-shaped, flimsy fronds which arise at regular intervals from the chestnut-brown scaly rhizome. (6 in.–1 ft.).

DICKSONIA

These are usually referred to as 'the' tree ferns. Like *Cyathea* they are only a short-term proposition for the small greenhouse owner, although in favoured parts of the country they often reach majestic proportions in the open. It is advisable to spray the trunks of these ferns daily with clear water during hot weather, because it is through the fibre and old frond bases that the young roots pass on their way from the crown to the base. Pot in John Innes No. 3 in pots which tend to be under-size, for all Dicksonias seem to do better when pot-bound. Propagation is by spores.

D. ANTARCTICA

The best known and most attractive species. Large feathery fronds with a tough, somewhat leathery, texture and bluish sheen are borne from the crown of a stout brownish trunk. (Up to 20 ft.).

D. FIBROSA

Golden Tree Fern. A medium-sized fern with yellowish fronds clothed in reddish-brown hairs and surmounting a strong columnar fibrous trunk. An admirable plant for the greenhouse since its rate of growth is relatively slow. Keep shaded from bright sunshine. (Up to 8 ft.).

D. LANATA

This delightful fern has a creeping rhizome as opposed to the more familiar trunk, and produces clusters of four or five fronds at irregular intervals. These are lance-shaped, light green above and much paler beneath. (3 ft.).

D. SQUARROSA

A fast-growing species with a slender black trunk. This is crowned with masses of beautiful yet roughly textured light green fronds, which may grow up to four feet long. By cutting the crown off the main trunk, large quantities of young plants can be induced to spring up from beneath the soil, thereby providing a rapid method of propagation. (Up to 12 ft.).

HYPOLEPIS

Fascinating ferns closely related to *Dennstaedtia* which can occasionally be obtained from specialist nurseries. By and large they are ferns for the warm greenhouse, but the three most popular species will do well in a cool house.

Left: Moisture-loving fern: *Onoclea sensibilis*
Right: the shade-loving *Athyrium filix-femina*
Below: the shade-loving *Polystichum setiferum*

Above: A cool-greenhouse fern, *Cyrtomium falcatum*
Below: A rock garden fern, *Gymnocarpium dryopteris*

H. BROOKSIAE

Long scrambling fronds, which appreciate some twiggy support pushed into their pots, arise from a thick rhizome, which is densely clothed in stiff brown hairs. The stems, or stipes, and rachis are a distinctive bluish colour and covered in small spiny outgrowths. Propagation is by spores or division of the creeping rootstock. (1–3 ft.).

H. MILLEFOLIUM

A handsome New Zealand native with attractive much divided fresh green fronds, which create a delightful filigree effect as they stand poised above the creeping rhizome on sturdy little three-inch-high stems. I find that this fern prefers a slightly acid free-draining compost and a position in full sun before giving of its best. Propagation is by spores or division. (6 in.–1 ft.).

H. RUGULOSA

(syn. *Dryopteris punctata*). An almost hardy species, with long creeping rhizomes that are densely covered in reddish-brown hairs. The fronds which grow from the rhizome at fairly regular intervals are roughly triangular, greenish-yellow, with stems that are similarly clothed in reddish hairs. Propagation is by spores or division. (6 in.–2 ft.).

LASTREOPSIS

Ferns similar in appearance to *Dryopteris*. Although mostly of tropical origin and currently difficult to obtain, the following are occasionally stocked by nurserymen and agreeably tolerant of cool house conditions. Propagation is by division of the rhizomes.

L. HISPIDA

Green or yellowish rather coarse almost triangular fronds

with very hairy stems. These grow from a long creeping rhizome that is densely clothed in bronze or coppery scales. Plant in pots of a gritty neutral or slightly acid compost and stand in heavy shade. Careful watering is the key to success with this species for it will not stand waterlogging or even perpetual dampness. (1–2 ft.).

L. PARISHII

A slightly more tender plant than the preceding, but one which can be grown fairly successfully under cool conditions, because it conveniently dies down and becomes dormant during the tricky winter months. The fronds are more succulent than in *L. hispida*. Grow in a well-drained alkaline soil in partial shade, drying the plant off completely during the winter. (9 in.–1 ft.).

LEPTOLEPIA

Splendid little ferns for the cool greenhouse or alpine house. I have come across only one in cultivation.

L. NOVAE-ZELANDIAE

Elegant broadly lance-shaped fronds with slightly scaly stalks, or stipes, arise from a slender creeping rhizome. Grow in a well-drained but slightly peaty compost. Easily propagated by allowing the rhizomes to creep out of the pot and root into other pots of peaty compost placed adjacent to the parent. These can be detached as separate plants as soon as the rhizome has rooted into the fresh compost. (1–2 ft.).

LEPTOPTERIS

New Zealand Crêpe Ferns. A group of very delicate and temperamental ferns which are usually too difficult for the average amateur to manage without special conditions, but one is so exotic and beautiful as to be worth a try.

L. SUPERBA

Prince of Wales Feather. One of the finest cool-greenhouse ferns. A real gem, with dark green translucent, almost membraneous, fronds that may be up to three feet long, and clothed along underside with distinctive woolly hairs. The fronds are produced symmetrically around a short trunk that seldom exceeds two feet in height. Difficult to establish in the open greenhouse unless gently sprayed overhead with tepid soft water four or five times a day. I prefer to enclose this species in a Wardian Case or frame constructed within the greenhouse so that humidity can be controlled with a greater degree of accuracy. Ordinary John Innes No. 3 compost seems to suit it, the pots being plunged in a bed of damp peat to help retain the moisture, in a shady part of the greenhouse. Propagation by spores is apparently not difficult, but I must confess that I have had little success to date. ($1\frac{1}{2}$–2 ft.).

MICROLEPIA

A family of worldwide distribution and closely allied to *Dennstaedtia*. Only one species is commonly cultivated in the cool greenhouse. Propagation is by spores.

M. SPELUNCAE

Broadly lance-shaped slightly hairy soft green fronds arise in a dense cluster from a hairy creeping rhizome. There are several varieties such as 'Hancei' and 'Villosissima', which differ basically in the distribution of minute hairs on the fronds. All are in cultivation and can be easily spotted by careful observation. They grow satisfactorily in John Innes compost No. 3 in a partially shaded position. (1–$2\frac{1}{2}$ ft.).

MICROSORIUM

Generally speaking these are epiphytic ferns from the higher regions of tropical Africa and Asia, although one species might be considered to be aquatic or at least amphibious, and generally unsuited to cultivation.

M. DIVERSIFOLIUM

(syn. *Polypodium diversifolium*). The only species commonly obtainable and probably the easiest to grow. Its fronds are a glossy dark green and somewhat reminiscent of the British native Polypody, *Polypodium vulgare*. They arise from a bluish-green rhizome which creeps across the surface of the compost. When potting be sure that it lies on the surface; burying it will almost certainly result in instant death. I like to use a compost composed of equal parts sphagnum moss, old leaves and fibrous loam and pot the plants into shallow pans. Propagation can easily be effected by pegging down the rhizome until it has become well rooted and then detaching and potting separately. (6 in.–1 ft.).

PELLAEA

These small-growing mountain ferns are easily accommodated in a cool greenhouse. Most could probably be tried outside in a sheltered garden with reasonable success. Indeed *P. atro-purpurea*, that was hitherto thought to be tender, is now a frequent occupant of sunny niches on the open rock garden. All species grow well in John Innes compost No. 3, with ample amounts of grit added to ensure quick drainage. Propagation is by spores.

P. FALCATA

A delightful little fern with a stout scaly rhizome from which are produced lance-shaped simple fronds with sickle-shaped leaflets. In its juvenile state this species is often confused with *P. rotundifolia*. (9 in.–1 ft.).

P. HASTATA

(syn. *P. calomelanos*). The largest *Pellaea* commonly grown. Its stipes, or frond stalks, are dark brown, erect growing and support large olive-green leaflets. I find that old plants tend to die out during the winter unless watered very carefully, and so I keep a regular propagation programme going so that there are always young ones coming along to serve as replacements. (1–2 ft.).

P. ROTUNDIFOLIA

An attractive little fern with slender wiry stems that carry alternate pairs of rounded pinnaea, or leaflets, along its full length. These are often slightly hairy or downy beneath and consequently do not like to be splashed or sprayed with water, particularly in the winter months. (6–9 in.).

PTERIS

Brake Ferns. One of the most popular groups of ferns for house plant treatment. They are almost evergreen, quite un-demanding and seem to thrive on neglect. Nomenclature is a little confused, but the bulk of the popular kinds are derived directly from the Cretan Brake, *Pteris cretica*. Propagation by spores is for the most part speedy and easy.

P. ARGUTA

Short-growing compact plant with wispy pale green fronds that are attractively variegated with silver. (9 in.–1 ft.).

P. ARGYRAEA

Very similar to the above, but with broad divided fronds with a similar silver variegation. (9 in.–1 ft.).

P. CRETICA

Cretan Brake. An almost hardy species which is frequently used as a centrepiece in bowls of forced hyacinths at Christmastime. The fronds consist of a long stem which spreads at the top into broad finger-like leaflets. Grow in ordinary John Innes No. 3 compost in either sun or shade. (1–2½ ft.).

P. CRETICA ALBO-LINEATA

Ribbon Brake. Identical to the common type, but with broad yellowish streaks running the length of the frond and its leaflets. Very popular on account of its easy-going nature. (1–2½ ft.).

P. C. CRISTATA

The fronds of this variety are the same as those of the ordinary Cretan Brake but with extensive terminal crests on the leaflets. (1–1½ ft.).

P. C. MAJOR

An improved and slightly enlarged version of *P. cretica*. (1–3 ft.).

P. C. MAYI

Narrow slender finger-like leaflets with attractive terminal crests and a conspicuous central streak of silver down each division are the principal attractions of this plant. I like to push a few twigs in the pot amongst the fronds of this variety for I find that without some kind of support it tends to become top-heavy and sprawl in all directions. (1–2 ft.).

P. C. RIVERTONIANA

Riverton Brake. Exceedingly attractive fronds that are heavily ruffled and lobed. (1–2 ft.).

P. C. WIMSETTII

Wimsett Brake. Neat-growing green leafed form with attractively tasselled and crested leaflets. (1–1½ ft.).

P. ENSIFORMIS

Sword Brake. This always looks to me like a narrower fronded but slightly taller version of *P. cretica*. Grow in John Innes No. 3 compost in partial shade. (1–3 ft.).

P. E. EVERGEMIENSIS

A shorter plant with striking silver variegated fronds. (1–2 ft.).

P. E. SIEBOLDII

An outstanding ruffled variety with two distinctive sets of fronds. The fertile ones are tall narrow and upright, whilst the barren ones are dwarf broad and spreading. (1–2 ft.).

P. E. VICTORIAE

A splendid plant with dark green fronds that are banded with yellow and white. (1–2 ft.).

P. SERRULATA

(syn. *P. Multifida*). Spider Brake. Very narrow and wispy fronds, like a much divided *P. cretica*. Grow in John Innes No. 3 compost in either sun or shade. (1–2 ft.).

P. S. CRISTATA

A very fine crested form. (1–2 ft.).

P. S. NANA

Although seldom encountered nowadays, this diminutive form was very popular some years ago and may occasionally be located in old gardens. A first class and really worthwhile plant. (6–9 in.).

P. S. VARIEGATA

The white and green variegated version of the common Spider Brake. (1–2 ft.).

P. TREMULA

A strong-growing green fronded species with untypical fronds. Whereas most species are divided into single finger-like projections, those of this plant are more finely divided and give a broadly lance-shaped outline to the entire frond. (1–2 ft.).

P. UMBROSA

Broad shiny dark green fronds arranged in dense masses around the crown. I think that this is probably the best variety of cool house fern for using as a foil for gaudy flowering subjects like Fuchsias and Begonias. Grow in either sun or shade in John Innes No. 3 compost. (1–2 ft.).

P. U. BERLIN

A selected, much improved market variety that is not too infrequently encountered in florists' shops nowadays. (1–2 ft.).

9

Warm-greenhouse Ferns

For the gardener who is fortunate enough to possess a warm greenhouse (minimum temperature 45–50 °F.), there are a whole host of exotic ferns to try. Many, it is true, are difficult to sustain without the aid of a Wardian Case, but there are sufficient different forms, shapes and sizes comparatively easy to cultivate currently available to satisfy even the most discriminating gardener. All the plants mentioned here fall into the latter category, and although some may be a little difficult to procure it is to be hoped that by mentioning them here they may become better known and that the various nurserymen who specialize in ferns are sufficiently pressed by inquiries to cause them to stock these beautiful but forgotten plants.

ADIANTUM

Maidenhair Ferns. It is generally conceded that the Maidenhairs are the most graceful and elegant species for a warm greenhouse. Most are reasonably easy to grow provided that they are shaded from bright sunlight. Propagation is usually by spores, although division is sometimes successful.

A. CAUDATUM

Trailing Maidenhair. An attractive plant for a hanging basket. When grown in a pot its slender soft green fronds often root and produce plantlets at their tips. It prefers a slightly alkaline soil. (9 in.–1½ ft.).

A. CUNEATUM

This is a Brazilian native with broadly triangular, delicate and extremely decorative fronds. Easily grown and frequently sold as a house plant. The various hybrid forms are far superior to the common type. (1–1½ ft.).

A. C. DEFLEXUM

Very similar in shape and form to the species, but with pinnules that are deflexed, giving the entire frond a strange but fascinating drooping appearance. (1–1½ ft.).

A. C. GRACILLIMUM

An extremely fine, much divided variety with fronds like clouds of green filigree. A useful subject for basket work. A very fine form listed as *A. c. gracillimum micropinnulum* with bronze or yellowish juvenile fronds is said to be superior, but I have not seen this. (1½–2 ft.).

A. C. GRANDICEPS

Another variety which can be accommodated successfully in a hanging basket. The fronds are long, with rather weak stipes, or frond stalks, and have heavily crested and tassellated ends which weigh them down. (1–1½ ft.).

A. C. LEGRANDII

Dwarf and much daintier version of *A. c.* 'Pacottii'. The pinnules are much smaller and more distantly placed. (9 in.).

A. C. PACOTTII

A small bushy plant with fronds that consist of masses of broad overlapping pinnules, which give the plant a stout solid appearance. (1–1½ ft.).

A. FLABELLULATUM

A small species with narrow fan-like finely divided fronds. Grow in a gritty well-drained compost. (9 in.).

A. PUBESCENS

Handsome glaucous fronds simply divided into a fan of separate digit-like portions. Each division bears legions of broad blunted pinnules in opposite pairs along the rachis. (1–2 ft.).

A. SOBOLIFERUM

This little fern appreciates a pinch of crushed chalk in its compost. A native of the Malayan region, it produces tufts of spreading soft green fronds on shiny black stipes. (1–1½ ft.).

A. TENERUM

What might be termed a 'typical Maidenhair'. Soft green, broadly triangular, much divided fronds with shiny black stipes, or frond stalks. (1–1½ ft.).

A. T. SCUTUM ROSEUM

A slightly larger form with new growth of a delightful shade of rose pink. (1–1½ ft.).

A. TRAPEZIFORME

The most graceful tropical species. Handsome drooping fronds of dull green diamond-shaped leaflets. Appreciates a little more heat than its cousins. (1–1½ ft.).

ASPLENIUM

Spleenworts. Several of the tropical species respond well to greenhouse culture if kept moist and shaded from bright sunshine.

A. ADIANTOIDES

A splendid little tufted fern with dull green broad simple fronds. In the wild it clings to moist rocks by means of its short creeping rhizome, conditions difficult to simulate in the artificial environs of a glasshouse, but I find that it does well in a shallow pan of compost consisting of equal parts loam, crushed sandstone and flint grit. Keep regularly sprayed overhead with soft water during warm weather. Propagation is by spores. (1–2 ft.).

A. CAUDATUM

Enormous olive-green fronds arise from a short rhizome clothed with distinctive long and narrow dark brown scales. Grow in moist peaty compost in shallow pans. (2–4 ft.).

A. MACROPHYLLUM

Almost identical to *A. adiantoides*, but with broader pinnae that are not lobed but regularly toothed. Cultivation is the same as for the latter and propagation by spores. (1 ft.).

A. NIDUS

Bird's-nest Fern. Probably too well known to need description. The broad machete-shaped fronds are arranged in a shuttlecock fashion around a central core of stem. This species is normally an epiphyte on the branches of trees, where it collects all manner of old leaves and debris which are converted into an effective growing medium. But in the greenhouse it does well in a compost of equal parts peat and loam in fairly pot-bound conditions. Keep shaded from intense sunlight, spray overhead twice daily during the summer, and feed regularly with liquid manure. I find that the manure commonly advocated for tomatoes is ideal. Propagation by spores. (1–3 ft.).

A. TENERUM

The fronds of this species look very much like a refined version of the common Polypody, *Polypodium vulgare*. They arise from a thick spongy rootstock which is thickly covered in black scales. Treat in the same manner as *A. nidus*. Propagation is by spores. (1 ft.).

A. UNILATERALE

A small fern with lance-shaped much divided fronds with distinctive purplish stems, or stipes, arising from a slender creeping rhizome. Grow in John Innes compost No. 3 with a little lime added and keep continually moist. Propagation is by spores. (6 in.–1 ft.).

ATHYRIUM

Lady Ferns. Although there are many tropical species suitable for cultivation under glass, lamentably few are commonly available to the gardening public. Broadly speaking cultivation should be along the lines of that advocated for the common Lady Fern, *A. filix-femina*, but with greater care taken over shading from strong sunlight.

A. ASPERUM

Probably the commonest tropical species. Long lance-shaped pale green fronds with prickly stipes grow from a stout woody rootstock that in old plants may assume the proportions of a trunk. Grow in John Innes compost No. 3, watering freely during the summer but only sparingly during winter. Propagation is by spores or division. (1–2 ft.).

A. CORDIFOLIUM

A chunky little fern with broadly lance-shaped, almost triangular, dull green fronds. In most plants these remain simply divided, but sometimes older specimens produce slightly larger and more complex fronds. Pot in John Innes compost No. 3 and stand in partial shade. Propagation is by spores. (1 ft.).

A. TOMENTOSUM

A bold upright plant with dull green slightly hairy fronds that grow from a short woody rootstock. The fronds are rather thick and coarse and vary considerably from plant to plant. Pot in John Innes compost No. 3 and keep well watered. Propagation is by spores. (1–2 ft.).

BLECHNUM

Handsome evergreen ferns which seem to grow well in either sun or shade but only in a very acid compost. John Innes compost without the base fertilizer but with a pinch of dried blood added seems to suit them admirably.

B. CILIATA

A similar but more refined version of *B. gibbum*. Propagation is by spores. (1–1½ ft.).

B. FINLAYSONIANUM

An extraordinary species which until now I have only persuaded to produce juvenile foliage. This is of simple structure, solid and broad like that of the Hart's Tongue Fern. Apparently the adult foliage is larger, leathery, and more characteristically divided. Propagation is by spores. (1–1½ ft.).

B. GIBBUM

(Syn. *Lomaria gibba*). This is the very popular species which is often grown in large quantities for sale as house plants, and marketed under its old name of *Lomaria gibba*. The fronds are leathery, dark green and broadly lance-shaped, and arise from a stout woody rootstock. Propagation is by spores. (1–1½ ft.).

B. ORIENTALE

One of the best greenhouse ferns for a hot sunny position. Its handsome dark green leathery fronds are reminiscent of those of its hardy counterpart, *B. spicant*. Propagation is by spores. (1–2 ft.).

CIBOTIUM

A small genus of tree ferns easy to grow. They appreciate a little shade and a rich leafy compost in crowded pot-bound conditions. I know of only two which are commonly available.

C. BAROMETZ

This is a short Malayan species with a creeping prostrate rootstock rather than a definite trunk, surmounted by a large tuft of soft green fronds that are densely clothed in shiny brown hairs when in their juvenile state. Propagation is by spores. (4 ft.).

C. SCHIEDEI

Mexican Tree Fern. A much taller species, up to ten feet high under glasshouse conditions, with graceful curving much divided light green fronds. Propagation is by spores.

DORYOPTERIS

Charming little creeping ferns with hard leathery fronds that are easy to grow in the greenhouse. They used to be classified as *Pteris* and some old gardeners still refer to them as this.

D. PEDATA

The commonest species, with dark green almost star-like fronds that are borne on stout wiry stems. Grow in a slightly alkaline compost. John Innes No. 3 with a pinch of hydrated lime added is admirable. Propagation is by spores. (1–1½ ft.).

GLEICHENIA

A genus of sun-loving ferns which could well be likened in stature, abundance and distribution to the common Bracken of temperate regions. Grow in John Innes compost No. 3, supporting the fronds with an arrangement of sticks pushed into the pot.

G. LINEARIS

Resam. A vigorous and ungainly yet fascinating plant. The fronds are long and branching, and consist of several fan-like sprays of deeply divided leaflets. The rhizome is slender and covered with reddish-brown hairs, and spreads rapidly around and across the pot, rooting into adjacent pots if not carefully watched. Propagation is by spores or division of the rhizomes. (1–4 ft.).

HEMIONITIS

Small ferns of similar appearance to *Doryopteris* but with more flexible slightly hairy fronds. All are essentially rock plants and easily grown in shallow pans of gritty compost.

H. ARIFOLIA

This is the one I usually grow and consider to be the best. It has a short tuft of dark green slightly hairy simple fronds which grow into quite a substantial mound of foliage. I find it essential to keep water from falling directly onto the foliage

Cool-greenhouse ferns: *Pteris ensiformis evergemiensis*
Pteris cretica albo-lineata

Cool-greenhouse fern:
Pteris serrulata 'Cristata'

Warm-greenhouse fern:
Platycerium alcicorne

because this causes unsightly brown blotches to appear. Propagation is by spores or division. (6–9 in.).

LYGODIUM

Although many of the very lovely species of tropical climbing fern are seldom encountered outside botanic gardens and public parks, those that are available are exceedingly rewarding and fascinating to grow. They all do well in John Innes compost No. 3 when allowed plenty of root run. Support should be given in the early stages of growth either by pushing sticks into the pots or training the young growths up wires stretched along the sides and roof of the greenhouse. All species grow easily from spores.

L. CIRCINNATUM

An easily grown plant with both fertile and sterile fronds. The sterile fronds are fan-shaped and broader than their fertile counterparts. In full sunlight both types of frond are produced but in shady situations only the sterile ones are in evidence. (2–3 ft.).

L. DIGITATUM

Very similar to the preceding, differing only in the size of leaflets, which in this case are considerably smaller. (2–3 ft.).

L. JAPONICA

A splendid vigorous fern with broad bright green palmate fronds. I usually cut the fronds right back to the ground on alternate years to give the plant a fresh start. (2–8 ft.).

L. SCANDENS

Almost lance-shaped fronds which are larger than those of the more typical *Lygodium* species and often hang from the climbing rachis. (2–4 ft.).

MARATTIA

A group of ancient ferns which have hardly evolved during the past five or six million years. The rhizomes are very distinctive, being extremely large in comparison with the fronds, and covered in masses of old frond bases. Easily grown in John Innes compost No. 3 if kept continually moist and in a shaded part of the greenhouse.

M. SALICINA

Horseshoe Fern. This noble New Zealand native deserves a place in every greenhouse collection. The fronds are dark green shiny and borne in large tufts on a curious woody rootstock. Apparently the rootstock makes good eating, and formed part of the diet of the early Maoris. Propagation is by spores. (1–4 ft.).

NEPHROLEPIS

Ladder Ferns. Comparatively easily grown and very ornamental ferns. As mentioned earlier, the majority of these respond well to basket culture. Numerous varieties with only slight differences of frond form are in cultivation, but all seem worthy of greenhouse space. Propagation of all kinds is easily effected by spores and many also respond favourably to division of the crowns.

N. BOSTONIENSIS

Boston Fern. Lace Fern. An exceedingly beautiful fern originally found growing amongst plants of *N. exaltata* in a nursery bed, and almost certainly a variety of that species. The graceful drooping fronds are very finely divided and in many reselected cultivar forms resemble moss. These arise from a short hard rootstock which often throws out underground runners that push up clusters of young fronds at regular intervals. Pot in John Innes compost No. 3 and keep in a shady part of the greenhouse. (1–3 ft.).

Following extensive work in both the United States and Holland, over a hundred different varieties have been raised, of which the following are the most freely available.

GLORIOSA

A compact version of 'Whitmanni'. (9 in.–1½ ft.).

MAASSII

Another compact variety but with very fine light green fronds. (1–1½ ft.).

ROOSEVELTII

Dark green mossy fronds which on established plants will grow up to three feet long and tumble right over the edge of the pot, hiding it completely from view. (2–4 ft.).

ROOSEVELTII PLUMOSA

Refined plumose form of the above. (1–3 ft.).

TEDDY

Differs little from the typical *N. bostoniensis* in structure but is much more compact and consequently better suited to greenhouse or living-room cultivation. (1–1½ ft.).

WHITMANNI

Very finely feathered and fringed pale green fronds. Probably the most popular commercial variety. (1–2 ft.).

N. CORDIFOLIA

Handsome pea-green lance-shaped fronds with narrow somewhat wiry stems, or stipes. Most of the plants I have seen in cultivation have been sterile and therefore propagated by division or offsets. (1–2 ft.).

N. C. COMPACTA

I have had this endearing little fern only for a couple of years, but during this time it has formed a sizable colony of plants which are complete miniature replicas of *N. cordifolia*, but perhaps with more coarsely divided fronds. (9 in.).

N. EXALTATA

Sword Fern. This is the largest *Nephrolepis* commonly grown. Its striking deep green upright fronds may reach a height of four feet or so and are very crispy and brittle.

N. HIRSUTULA

A delightful small species with pale green crimpled lance-shaped fronds. Easily confused with *N. exaltata* in the early stages of growth. (9 in.–1 ft.).

PLATYCERIUM

Stag's-horn Ferns. The habits of growth and method of cultivation of these remarkable epiphytes have been mentioned in an earlier chapter. I think it is sufficient to say here that no collection of ferns, however small, can be said to be complete or representative without at least one of these extraordinary plants. Propagation of all species is by spores, which are treated like those of a terrestrial species until large enough to be comfortably handled.

P. ALCICORNE

Probably the most popular species. Makes an excellent house plant on account of its tolerance of treatment as an ordinary terrestrial species when planted in a leafy or peaty compost. Its simply divided fronds are greyish-green when young but become brown and parchment-like with age.

P. ANDINUM

Fairly coarse green pendulous fronds which are divided and subdivided into pairs of equal leaflets each with a V-shaped terminal cleft.

P. CORONARIUM

A fast-growing plant with sterile upright greyish-green basket-like fronds and long pendulous divided fertile ones.

P. GRANDE

A bold and stately species which produces an enormous upright basket of greyish spreading fronds. I prefer to grow this in a pan of leafy compost rather than on a piece of log, for it tends to become top heavy and ungainly.

P. VASSEI

A quite startling species which thrusts out glaucous sterile and fertile fronds in all directions. Usually rather expensive but well worth obtaining when the opportunity arises.

P. WALLICHII

I must confess to never having grown this one, but I have seen it looking very happy under cultivation. Broad upright basket fronds almost as wide as long surmount the scaly remains of the previous fronds. From amidst these the repeatedly branched pendulous grey-green fertile ones are produced.

POLYPODIUM

Many have been recommended in the past for the greenhouse, but most of these have now been renamed and classified under new or different genera and consequently will be found listed as such. One species, however, which has lingered under the old name can be highly recommended for both greenhouse and living-room cultivation.

P. AUREUM

A very attractive plant with masses of gorgeous blue-green fronds each sprinkled beneath with clusters of golden spore cases. (1–3 ft.).

P. A. MANDAIANUM

This form has ruffled and crimpled leaflets but is otherwise identical to the preceding. Both are propagated by spores. (1–3 ft.).

SELAGINELLA

While this group of plants cannot be correctly called ferns, they do deserve a mention here because they are invariably treated as such. All like moist shady conditions and thrive in pans of damp gritty compost, which they rapidly colonize with their attractive mossy foliage. *Selaginella martensii*, with green and silvery foliage, is the most popular, although there are upwards of a dozen different kinds commonly available from nurserymen and florists.

SOCIETIES

Most groups of plants have their ardent band of admirers who have at some time met together to form a society to foster the interests of their particular subject. Ferns are no exception, and I would suggest that any gardener who intends taking his plants seriously should subscribe to at least one of those mentioned, for it is only by comparing notes and experiences with fellow members that a complete knowledge and mastery of the subject can be gained. In addition it is also a good common ground on which to meet fellow fern-lovers socially. Indeed some of my closest friends were first encountered during meetings or through correspondence within the following societies.

THE BRITISH PTERIDOLOGICAL SOCIETY

A very old society formed at Kendal in 1891. Its purpose is to instruct and disseminate information amongst its members on the cultivation and botany of ferns and allied plants. Both botanically and horticulturally orientated enthusiasts belong and are catered for admirably by the society's publications. The more botanically minded appreciate *The British Fern Gazette* which appears annually, whilst those like myself with a more horticultural outlook derive much enjoyment from the substantial newsletters which arrive at regular intervals. Excursions, indoor meetings and other activities are arranged at various times throughout the year and are most enjoyable. Details are available from the Secretary, Mr J. W. Dyce, 46 Sedley Rise, Loughton, Essex, or c/o the British Museum (Natural History) Botany Department, South Kensington, London S.W.7.

AMERICAN FERN SOCIETY

A lively society open to all those interested in the study and cultivation of ferns. Details from Smithsonian Institution, Washington D.C., U.S.A.

LOS ANGELES INTERNATIONAL FERN SOCIETY

A worldwide organization which issues monthly newsletters and has a spore distribution scheme. Full details from: Wilbur W. Olson, Membership Chairman, 13715 Cordary Ave., Hawthorne, California 90250.

THE MALAYAN NATURE SOCIETY

Although not strictly a fern society, this one does cater admirably for those with interests in tropical ferns native to the Malayan region. Publications are not too technical, but are based on botany and ecology rather than cultivation. Details from: The Secretary, P.O. Box 750, Kuala Lumpur, Malaya.

NELSON NEW ZEALAND FERN SOCIETY

A friendly society formed in 1933 with the expressed intention of 'exchanging knowledge and experience on fern growing'. Full details are available from Miss K. H. Stocker, Mapua, Via Nelson, New Zealand.

JAPANESE PTERIDOLOGICAL SOCIETY

A national society whose existence has only recently come to my notice and therefore renders me unable to comment fairly on its activities. Details from Dr K. Iwatsuki, Department of Botany, Faculty of Science, Kyoto University, Kyoto, Japan.

THE NIPPON FERNIST CLUB

A large and active Japanese society that welcomes contact with both amateur and professional foreign pteridologists. Further information from Mr Tomitaro Namegata, 481 Narita, Narita-shi, Chiba-ken, Japan 286.

GLOSSARY

ALTERNATE. Arranged alternately on either side of the axis.

AXIS. Central part of the frond about which the leafy portion is arranged.

BULBIL. Small bulb-like buds which appear on the fronds of several species.

DECIDUOUS. Plants with foliage that falls in the autumn or when they are in poor condition.

EPIPHYTE. A plant which clings to a tree as other host for support but does not derive any nourishment directly from it.

FROND. The entire fern leaf.

GLABROUS. Smooth, hairless.

GLAND. An organ which secretes a fluid which is usually beneficial to the plant.

GLAUCOUS. Tinged with blue.

INDUSIUM. The membrane protecting the sorus.

LOBE. A shallow, usually rounded, segment.

MUTANT. A plant which differs from its parents as a result of genetical change, usually without any visible external influence.

PINNAE. The primary division of a fern frond.

PINNULE. The secondary or ultimate divisions of a frond.

PROTHALLUS. A minute green scale arising from the germination of a spore.

PTERIDOPHYTES. The class of higher flowerless plants which embraces all the fern species.

RACHIS. The axis of a compound frond, excluding the stalk.

SORUS. A group of sporangia.

SPORANGIUM. Capsule containing spores.

SPORE. A tiny one-celled body like a pollen grain which, on germination, gives rise to a prothallus.

SPOROPHYTE. The spore-bearing or adult generation of a fern.

STIPE. The frond stalk.

VENATION. Arrangement of the veins in a leaflet.

FERN NURSERIES

GREENHOUSE FERNS

Thomas Butcher, Wickham Road Nursery, Shirley, near Croydon, Surrey.

HARDY FERNS

Noel Brookfield, 102 Stamford Road, Birkdale, Southport, Lancs.
Highfields Nursery, Caldecote, Cambridge.
Highlands Water Gardens, Rickmansworth, Herts.
Hillier and Sons, Winchester, Hants.
Reginald Kaye Ltd, Waithman Nurseries, Silverdale, Carnforth, Lancs.
Lochhall Nursery, 21–3 Kirk Street, Stonehouse, Larkhall, Lanarkshire.
Newlake Gardens, New Chapel Road, Crawley, Sussex.
Perrys Hardy Plant Farm, Theobalds Park Road, Enfield.
Proudley's Heather Nursery, Two Bridges, Blakeney, Glos.
Sunningdale Nurseries, Windlesham, Surrey.

ROCK GARDEN FERNS

W. E. Th. Ingwersen Ltd, Birch Farm Nursery, Gravetye, East Grinstead, Sussex.

INDEX